PENGUIN BUSINESS
YOU CAN COMPOUND

Vivek Mashrani is the founder and director at Technofunda Ventures, based out of Ahmedabad. He has previously worked at the Bengaluru and London offices of HSBC as an associate vice president of their investment banking and strategy teams. Vivek is a chartered financial analyst (CFA) charter holder and member of the CFA Society India as well as an MBA in capital markets from Narsee Monjee Institute of Management Studies, Mumbai. He is a strong believer in lifelong learning, networking and collaboration, and is also building an investing community under his TechnoFunda initiative to help people become better investors. Vivek is also the author of the bestselling book *Action: 100 Powerful Principles of Personal Finance* (2024).

DISCLAIMER

All stocks discussed should be considered examples and case studies for academic purposes only. These are not recommendations to buy/sell.

Please consult your own financial advisor before taking any financial decision based on this book.

Views on individual stocks and/or sectors could have changed or can change at any point of time. Please do your due diligence from time to time.

YOU CAN COMPOUND

Secrets, Strategies
and Frameworks
to Make Money by
Investing in Stocks

VIVEK MASHRANI

PENGUIN
BUSINESS

An imprint of Penguin Random House

PENGUIN BUSINESS

Penguin Business is an imprint of the Penguin Random House group of companies
whose addresses can be found at global.penguinrandomhouse.com

Published by Penguin Random House India Pvt. Ltd
4th Floor, Capital Tower 1, MG Road,
Gurugram 122 002, Haryana, India

First published by Penman Books 2022
Published in Penguin Business by Penguin Random House India 2024

ISBN 9780143463672

Typeset in Sabon LT Std by Manipal Technologies Limited, Manipal
Printed at Replika Press Pvt. Ltd, India

www.penguin.co.in

CONTENTS

PART 3: REFINE

TO DOWNLOAD FREE BONUSES visit:
http://youcancompound.com/

PART 1
LEARN

CHAPTER ONE

GOLDMINE TO CREATE WEALTH

"The trouble with being in the rat race is that even if you win, you're still a rat."
—Lily Tomlin

Chatur Champak and Rocking Ranjita are a happily married Indian middle-class couple. Chatur worked in an IT Services company as a project manager, and Ranjita was a homemaker. The initial few years were fantastic - frequently ordering food from outside, buying the latest gadgets, partying on weekends and vacationing in exotic destinations twice a year.

Their life was like a plain sail until they entered a new phase of life: parenting. This awakened them to a new reality of life. The same salary that was enough to live a classy lifestyle now looked deflated. One Sunday morning, when the Chatur and Ranjita calculated what they had in the name of savings for their kid's future education, they were thunderstruck. They realized they had pint-sized savings resting in their account. A major portion of Chatur's income leaked into paying credit card bills, rent, EMIs, grocery, rent and other bills. To add insult to the injury, he received a salary hike of not more than 4-6% annually. For them, it was like trying to overtake a car rolling at twice their speed. They were now facing the brutal brunt of inflation.

It is a human tendency to toss the accountability on someone or the situation when entrapped in challenging times. Therefore, Ranjita blamed government policy, the external environment, low-interest rates, capitalism, etc., for all their hardships. She asked, "Aaj kal mein mehengai bahut badh gayi hai?" (hasn't inflation shot up too much these days?). I am sure this must be the case with a lot of us when we face the deterioration of purchasing power because of inflation.

Like a drowning man trying to catch at a straw, Chatur decided to seek help from this friend Ayran Azad. Chatur and Aryan studied in the same college and landed the same job. However, Aryan quit his job and start his venture after achieving financial freedom. So, Chatur invited him to dinner on the same weekend. As Ranjita was busy making preparations in the kitchen, the two friends started discussing their financial situations. Chatur explained that he was working hard at the office to keep his job and compete with colleagues, but still struggling to get a decent salary hike.

He further shared the financial mess he was caught in. After being all ears to Chatur, Aryan spotted many issues in his finances and explained those to him.

Aryan explained three significant issues:

1. Chatur was not saving enough. Only 5% of his net salary was going into savings.

2. He had invested his savings into FDs and some real estate property for the tax benefit, which was barely yielding a return of 3-5% post-tax returns.

3. Despite working hard, his salary barely rose by 4-5%, which could not keep up with much higher inflation rates to maintain the same lifestyle.

Aryan said, "You have fallen into a rat race, my dear friend. You are toiling hard for the money, but your money is not working hard for you. You are scarcely investing, and that return, too, is not beating inflation. So, at best, if you keep running like this, your standard of living will remain the same or even become worse."

With raised brows, Chatur immediately asked, "How can I come out of this deep well? What did you do to achieve your financial freedom? How can I become financially *aatmanirbhar* (independent)?"

After a brief pause, Aryan replied, "You are running on a hedonic treadmill; even though you are running hard, you are in the same place. Right now, you are working for money. Instead, it would be best if you made money work for you. Make money your slave, not your master."

The trouble with being in the rat race is that even if you win, you're still a rat.

You are working hard for the money, but your money is not working hard for you.

The book *Classics: An Investor's Anthology* features an essay about P.T. Barnum that rightly covers this aspect of the hedonic treadmill:

"Thousands of men are kept poor, and tens of thousands are made so after they have acquired enough to support them well through life, in consequence of laying their plans of living on an expensive platform...

Prosperity is a more severe ordeal than adversity, especially sudden prosperity. "Easy come, easy go" is an old and true proverb. Pride, when permitted full sway, is the great undying cankerworm which gnaws the very vitals of a man's worldly possessions, let them be small or great, hundreds or millions. *Many persons, as they begin to prosper, immediately commence expending for luxuries, until in a short time their expenses swallow up their income, and they become ruined in their ridiculous attempts to keep up appearances and make a "sensation" [emphasis added]."*[1]

Aryan continued, "Right now, the equation you are following is Income - Expenses = Savings. Instead, it should be Income - Savings = Expenses. This will change the way you think about money."

Warren Buffett has said, "If you don't find a way to make money while you sleep, you will work until you die." Hence, it is important to generate passive income.

Aryan then tapped on his phone and showed Chatur this quadrant:[2]

Employee	Business Owner
E	**B**
You <u>have</u> a job	You own a <u>system</u> & people work for you
Self Employed	Investor
S	**I**
You <u>own</u> a job	Money works for you

---

[1] Charles Ellis and James Vertin, *Classics: An Investor's Anthology* (New York: Business One Irwin, 1988)

[2] Chad Carson, https://www.coachcarson.com/cash-flow-quadrant-how-earn-matters/; Inspired from Robert Kiyosaki's book Cashflow Quadrant

Employee: This is how most people earn their income. You slog it out at the office from 9 to 5, grow your salary by 5-7% through hikes and promotions to cope with inflation, and earn money. The more you work, the more you earn, so you need to keep working to earn. The moment you stop working, your income goes to zero. This is not bad, but you can do better by working for yourself.

Self-employed: You run your independent practice like a doctor, lawyer or chartered accountant. Here too, the moment you stop working, your income goes to zero. But in this case, you have the flexibility of your work hours and you are not answerable to a 'boss'. This is better than a job, but not the best.

Business owner: In the first two quadrants (E and S), you worked for money. Now, others too are working for you. So, even if you stop working, your income will not drop to zero. This is a very good situation but still not ideal.

Investor: This is the 'dream come true'. This is how Warren Buffett built his massive fortune- by investing in other companies. We will soon learn more about this in greater detail.

Aryan quoted Sir Albert Einstein - "Compound interest is the eighth wonder of the world. He who understands it, earns it. He who doesn't, pays it." Aryan then continued, "Do you understand? Compounding is the aanthva ajuba (eighth wonder) of this world."

With curiosity hovering over his face, Chatur asked, "How does this work?" Like many of us, Chatur had learned about compound interest in his school, but mugged up the formula for the exams and did not understand its true power.

Aryan explained, "Let's say you have ₹200. You put ₹100 each in two different accounts. One with 10% simple interest, and the other with 10% compound interest. At the end of the first year, both accounts will have ₹110. But at the end of the second year, the simple interest account will have ₹120, while the compound interest account will have ₹121."

Chatur asked, "But this is such a small difference. Only one extra ₹ after two years?"

Aryan continued, "Wait and watch, my friend. Good things take time…"

Next what Aryan shared took Chatur by surprise and he kept staring at the bottom figures without batting an eyelid.

Years	Simple Interest 10%	Compound Interest 10%
1	110	110
2	120	121
3	130	133.1
4	140	146.4
5	150	161.1
6	160	177.2
7	170	194.9
8	180	214.4
9	190	235.8
10	200	259.4
11	210	285.3
12	220	313.8
13	230	345.2
14	240	379.7
15	250	417.7
16	260	459.5

Years	Simple Interest 10%	Compound Interest 10%
17	270	505.4
18	280	556.0
19	290	611.6
20	300	672.7
21	310	740.0
22	320	814.0
23	330	895.4
24	340	985.0
25	350	1083.5
26	360	1191.8
27	370	1311.0
28	380	1442.1
29	390	1586.3
30	400	1744.9

Now that you have understood the power of compounding, let's see what incremental compounding can do to your purchasing power.

If you invested 10K each month for 30 years, results:

5%- 15,00,000

15%- 24,36,000

25%- 40,00,000

As Morgan Housel explains in his excellent book *The Psychology of Money*, "Buffett is the richest investor of all time. But he's not actually the greatest—at least not when measured by average annual returns. Jim Simons, head of the hedge fund Renaissance Technologies, has compounded money at 66% annually since 1988. No one comes close to this record. As we just saw, Buffett has compounded at roughly 22% annually, a third as much. Simons' net worth, as I write, is $21 billion. He is—and I know how ridiculous this sounds given the numbers we're dealing with—75% less rich than Buffett. Why the difference if Simons is such a better investor? Because Simons did not find his investment stride until he was 50 years old. He's had less than half as many years to compound as Buffett. If James Simons had earned his 66% annual returns for the 70-year span Buffett has built his wealth he would be worth—please hold your breath—sixty-three quintillion nine hundred quadrillion seven hundred eighty-one trillion seven hundred eighty billion seven hundred forty-eight million one hundred sixty thousand dollars."

With a trail of questions surfacing one after another in Chatur's mind, he jawed another one, "But Warren Buffett started investing when he was 11 years old. I am already 35. How can I benefit from the power of compounding?"

Aryan leaned forward, forked out a slice of pineapple from the fruit bowl, tugged it into his mouth, and munched it slowly, feeling the tangy taste with closed eyes. Once done, he voiced, "Better earlier than later, but better late than never!"

Veteran investor Ramesh Damani has explained how you can turn 10 lakh into 100 crores in 30 years. You need only to double your money every three years, which works out to a 26% compounded return. In fact, 26% is such a golden number that Mohnish Pabrai has made a number plate of it!

Chatur said in amazement, "If I can compound by 25%, it would be a great journey in the next 30 years. I will become one among the top 1% of the richest people in the world if I have ₹ 100 crores. But the savings account gives 4 to 6% interest. Bonds give around 8 to 10%. Gold and real estate too yield around 10 to 12% returns. So how can I achieve 25%?"

Aryan replied with a smile, "Invest in businesses directly, or in equities through the stock market."

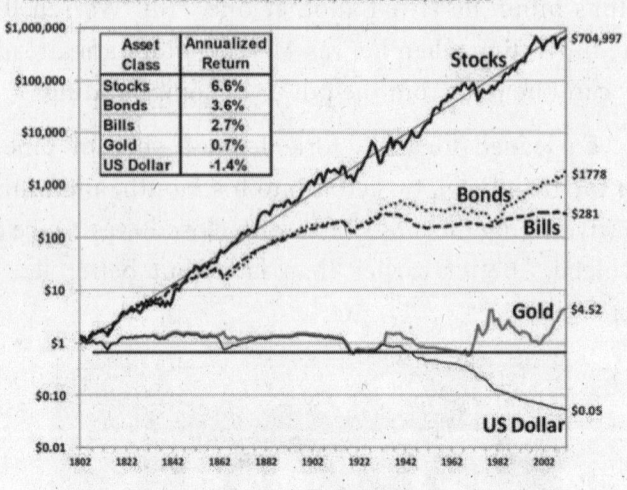

Total Real Returns on U.S. Stocks, Bonds, Bills, Gold, and the Dollar, 1802–2012

Asset Class	Annualized Return
Stocks	6.6%
Bonds	3.6%
Bills	2.7%
Gold	0.7%
US Dollar	-1.4%

Total Returns Comparison[3]

---

[3]Jeremy Siegel, *Stocks for the Long Run: The Definitive Guide to Financial*

Ranjita, who was all ears to the conversation from the kitchen, immediately questioned, "But isn't investing in the stock market the same as gambling your money?"

And then, Aryan explained a few more powerful principles.

Suppose your friend is doing business. He owns 100% of that company. Now he wants investors to invest in his company. Assume that he has 100 shares in this company, and you buy one share from him. Congratulations, you just became a 1% partner in that company. Similarly, when you buy shares of any company from stock markets, you become a part-owner of the business proportionate to the number of shares you purchase.

The power of investing is that if the business grows profitably, you also compound your money by investing in underlying companies. Peter Lynch has said- "Stocks aren't lottery tickets. Behind every stock is a company. If the company does well, over time the stocks do well, and vice versa. You have to look at the company—that's what you research."[4]

Immediately Chatur asked, "So instead of spending time starting my own business, I can invest in multiple businesses through the stock market?"

Market Returns & Long-Term Investment Strategies (New York: McGraw Hill, 1994)

[4]Lessons from an investing legend, https://www.fidelity.com/viewpoints/investing-ideas/peter-lynch-investment-strategy#:~:text=Lynch%3A%20Stocks%20aren't%20lottery,company%E2%80%94that's%20what%20you%20research

"Exactly!" Aryan replied. The stock market is even more beneficial than running your own business! You can be a part-owner of many businesses rather than owning just one.

Firstly, it gives you the flexibility of switching businesses at your own will. You can be the owner of an FMCG business today; you can be out and into a steel company tomorrow; you can switch into a pharmaceutical business the day after tomorrow. Do you have this versatility in the case of your own business?

Secondly, you have the option of having the brightest, most talented managers and businessmen, like Aditya Puri and N Chandrasekaran, working for your company, that too at no extra cost! Do you have this privilege when you run a business? Of course not!

Thirdly, you can run multiple businesses simultaneously. You can run a specialty chemicals business, a pharmaceutical business, an FMCG business, and a bank simultaneously! If you had to set up a chemicals factory yourself, it would cost many crores of ₹. However, you can purchase part-ownership stakes in listed chemical businesses for a few hundred ₹ by buying shares of the company on the stock exchange. This option of a small ticket size means you can run a conglomerate (i.e., your portfolio) for as low as a few thousand ₹!

Unlike your own business, you have no emotional attachment. Also, certain businesses like liquor, pharma and banks require regulatory approval and licenses. This is a very tedious and hectic job if you are running your own business, whereas, as an equity investor, you do not need to worry about this.

Closing and shutting down a business is difficult, but as an equity investor, you can simply sell your shares in a few clicks. Equity investing is also much more scalable, as a portfolio of 1 crore will not need significantly more monitoring than a portfolio of 10 lakhs. Whereas in a business, you will need to hire more employees, open a new factory, etc. to grow from 10 lakhs to 1 crore.

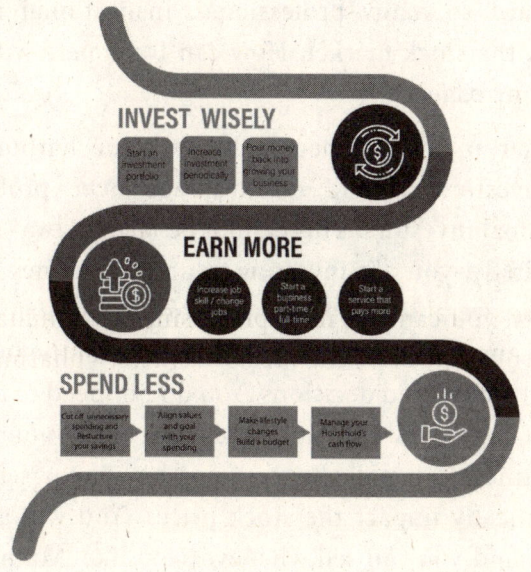

The stock market is also a place that offers you incredible bargains, like businesses for less than the cash in the bank, which is impossible in a private business. You also earn dividends as passive income, thus making your money work for you while you sleep.

Best of all, you don't need to go to the office! What can be better than being the owner of multiple businesses for a few thousand ₹, having top-notch professional managers working for your business, and relaxing in the comfort of your home? You can continue to earn through active income from your job or other means and keep deploying to generate your passive income, eventually becoming a full-time investor once you achieve financial independence.

Chatur was amazed. He said, "This is a fantastic way to earn passive income and make money work for me. But I have heard so many professional, institutional investors invest in the stock market. How can I compete with them? What is my edge?"

Another myth that people like Chatur harbor is that retail investors have a disadvantage over professional, institutional investors. This cannot be farther away from the truth! Firstly, you are investing your own money and you are not answerable to anyone else for your returns. You do not have any external pressure to outperform the indices, so you can take relaxed decisions. You do not need to chase the latest IPO or follow ESG norms, etc. Secondly, your amount of investment is small; hence, your buying or selling will not drastically impact the stock prices. You will also have liquidity and you can sell whenever you like. Mutual Funds (MFs) have extremely large holdings and if they wish to sell their stakes, the price will fall significantly. Institutional investors also have certain limitations; for example, a single stock cannot be beyond 10% of their portfolio. Hence, when you average up and add to your winning positions (more on this later in the book), MFs must sell their winners periodically! However, you, as a retail investor, do not have these restrictions. Mutual Funds need to gradually build up their positions, so they need to accumulate even when the stock is stagnant. On the contrary, you do not need to do this and can directly buy stocks when they are in stage 2, instead of holding in stage 1 (we will walk through stage 2 in more detail later in the book).

Another big disadvantage for funds or institutions is size. If you think about the size of the mutual fund, typically it can be anywhere between 1000 to several thousand crores. As a result, the universe of companies, which they can select out of 3000 to 4000 listed companies, gets narrowed down. The number of investable companies for institutions is very low, and is often restricted to large caps, which are relatively more efficiently priced than small caps.

Most fund managers are also risk-averse. As the classical adage goes, "Nobody gets fired for buying IBM." Similarly, nobody gets sacked for buying TCS or Infosys. But because their high-paying job is at stake, they are reluctant to buy a 700-crore market cap company, irrespective of its growth potential.

MFs also have constant scrutiny on insider trading, etc.

Besides, they must invest as a team. There are CIOs, fund managers, analysts, etc., and a senior CIO's opinion may not be disagreed with, because there is a job on the line! As Mohnish Pabrai has said, "Investing is not a team sport, it is more of an individual pursuit"[5]

When a news trigger comes and a promising opportunity appears, retailers can directly buy, but Mutual Funds cannot. They must create a report, get it approved through the

---

[5]https://www.youtube.com/watch?v=9tGjXPhnp-s&t=387s

internal committee, etc., and by the time they buy it, the stock may have already spiraled up significantly.

65 to 70% of mutual funds cannot beat the index consistently for the long term!

So, before you buy, ask yourself: Can I analyze the company? Everybody has a good idea of what McDonald's does. But it's hard to analyze biotechnology companies or computer software companies. Do you know something about the company? What can you add to the math? Do you have an edge?

You could be an interventional cardiologist, and you put in a heart pump. You say, wow, this is an incredible breakthrough, preventing shock and providing hemodynamic support. You are in the operating room, seeing this breakthrough way ahead of most people. That's an edge. You need an edge on something.[6]

Meanwhile, Ranjita ferried in a tray of snacks; the fragrance penetrating through the layer of air in the room and invading the olfactory sense of the two friends.

While popping in a cheese ball from the plate, Chatur exclaimed, "With all these advantages, I am guaranteed to make money!"

As he said this, he did not realize that the appetizer was piping hot, he instantly requested Ranjita to pour a glass of water to silence the aftereffect.

---

[6]https://www.fidelity.com/viewpoints/investing-ideas/peter-lynch-investment-strategy#:~:text=Lynch%3A%20Stocks%20aren't%20lottery,company%E2%80%94that's%20what%20you%20research

Watching Chatur rolling water in his mouth, Aryan tried to instill a realistic mindset in Chatur without killing his dopamine rush. "*Dost* (friend), in the stock market, there is no guarantee. It is all about probabilities. If there is a coin toss where the probability of heads and tails are both 50-50, and landing heads give you a 100 ₹, while landing tails yields only 50 ₹, that is also investing. Most important, you should keep the return expectations moderate. If other asset classes give 8 to 12% per annum returns, then the stock market can fetch you 15 to 18%. However, if you expect your money to double in six months, this is not the right place for you."

As Charlie Munger has said, "You're looking for a mispriced gamble. That's what investing is. And you have to know enough to know whether the gamble is mispriced. That's value investing."[7]

Chatur, now less euphoric, bombarded Aryan with his questions. "There are 5000+ companies; how can I select a few handfuls of stocks among these? How can I research companies and select which ones to invest in? How can I learn when to buy stocks and when to sell?"

Aryan, sensing Chatur's inquisitiveness, replied calmly, "Don't worry, my friend. I will answer all your questions before I bail out for the day."

Chatur added, "I am so excited to know the answers. My pulse is a race car!"

Investing is just like any other game, but not in a derogatory way. You play with the right discipline, mindset, ethics and

[7]Farnam Street (blog), https://fs.blog/charlie-munger-wisdom/

behaviors, and know the rules (processes/systems/tactics). Bet big when the odds are in your favor. But, unlike other games, investing is like a dice loaded in your favor. That is because, firstly, very few people play this game. Even more important, out of those who play this game, around half the people don't even understand the rules of the game! So, do you want to participate in this wonderful game? But, like every game, you also need to do your homework before playing.

Aryan chimed, "Let me share some remarkable examples and proven techniques with you that can answer most of your questions."

Ranjita intercepted, "But before that, let's appease our palate as the dinner is ready."

And the conversation continued as they feasted on the dessert over the dining table.[8]

Your task for this chapter is to find at least five companies that have given returns of 26% CAGR (100x in 20 years) or more in the last 20 years and share this list with me over email at *vivek@vivekmashrani.com* to get an awesome return gift. As Philip Fisher has said, "To make money, you need to understand how money was made in the past."

---

[8]Sources:

https://www.dr-mikes-math-games-for-kids.com/rice-and-chessboard.html

https://twitter.com/Sanjay__Bakshi/status/1329369171491135491

(https://www.youtube.com/watch?v=9tGjXPhnp-s&t=387s)

https://www.coachcarson.com/cash-flow-quadrant-how-earn-matters/

CHAPTER SUMMARY

- Financial intelligence is key. However, a story of a young, happily married couple (Chatur and Ranjita) has fallen into a rat race as, despite working hard, the money was not working for them.

- The reason the couple is struggling financially is their high-end lifestyle (regularly ordering food outside, going on exotic holidays, and buying fancy gadgets).

- With such a lifestyle and the high inflation, the couple's purchasing power deteriorates.

- Ranjita lacked financial intelligence and argues that the main causes for their suffering include capitalism, low-interest rates, and government policies.

- Chatur realized his mistakes and sought financial planning help from a long-term friend, Aryan, who seemed financially intelligent.

- In Chatur's expenditure and income story, Aryan picked three main things the couple was doing wrongly. They include:

  - Not saving enough- they saved only 5% of the net salary

  - Investing in FDs and real estate for tax benefits. Unfortunately, they received only 3-5% post-tax returns

  - Low salary growth of only 4-5%-such could not cater to higher inflation rates

- Living a high-end lifestyle mostly affects the saving plan. From Chatur's story, such a lifestyle resulted in them running on a hedonic treadmill (remaining at the same position even with his fast-running speed).

- Many adopt the following formula: income-expenses =savings. However, to effectively save and become financially independent, they should adopt the income-savings = expenses formula.

- Attaining financial freedom and independence requires one to make money as "a slave".

- Exploring various investors' lives, such as Buffett, veteran Ramesh Damani and James Simons, compounding makes one's money grow faster.

- Invest in businesses directly or in equities through the stock market.

- Compounding is not like gambling as many think. A good plan shields one from losing.

- Investing in the stock market is even more beneficial than owning a business. The benefits include:

  - Investing in many businesses at once

  - Flexibility to switch businesses

  - Benefit from the most talented managers' knowledge of business

  - Incredible gains are also noted as an individual expects to earn dividends from passive income where money works for someone

- In conclusion, investing is like any other game. However, one should play with the right ethics, know the rules, and have the right mindset and discipline.

YOUR REFLECTIONS

(Reflect on what you have learned and pen down your thoughts)

_____

_____

_____

_____

_____

_____

_____

_____

_____

_____

_____

_____

_____

_____

_____

_____

_____

_____

_____

_____

CHAPTER TWO
FINANCIAL FREEDOM FLYWHEEL

"It is important to view knowledge as sort of a semantic tree - make sure you understand the fundamental principles, i.e., the trunk and big branches, before you get into the leaves/ details or there is nothing for them to hang on to."[1]

—Elon Musk

The financial freedom flywheel concept inspired by Jeff Bezos, for Amazon, starts by recommending individuals to make a few adjustments, reevaluate their expenses, and save up a little more. According to this concept, individuals are encouraged to start saving for an investment, for example,

[1]Elon Musk, "I Am Elon Musk, CEO/CTO of a Rocket Company, AMA!" Reddit, 2015, https://www.reddit.com/r/IAmA/ comments/2rgsan/i_am_elon_musk_ceocto_of_a_rocket _company_ ama/?st=jg8ec825&sh=4307fa36

the stock market or elsewhere. The amount saved may not be huge, but developing the habit is the key element. Once the saving flywheel starts spinning, it gets easier to keep adding more velocity. Each step in the flywheel requires action and provokes the next one.

APPLYING AMAZON'S FLYWHEEL TO BECOME A GOOD INVESTOR

The platform Mega-Trend has become common in this day and age where businesses build online digital structures and enable human activities, including shopping and selling. Such a platform allows businesses to scale up even without owning assets. For example, Uber, the world's biggest ride-sharing company, does not own any cars. Airbnb, the largest accommodation provider, has no real estate. Lastly, Alibaba, one of the most valuable retailers, has no inventory.

What is the reason behind the success of these platform businesses? From Amazon's example, the flywheel model has been beneficial to them. In the flywheel illustration below, the first element that Amazon focuses on is the customer experience; by creating a solid platform, customers can browse easily. The second one is increasing the platform traffic (both customers and sellers). Every additional platform visitor or a customer can create more value for the existing ones. This traffic ensures that more products are listed on the platform, and once listed, they get customers. When satisfied customers write reviews, it encourages others to purchase from their platform. Bezos's second approach was to lower the cost of the structure, a major phenomenon in the platform business. These businesses require a good infrastructure that costs a lot, including high capital, to build the system. However, once this is done, with any incremental customer that comes in, the business can lower the prices while, at the same time, improving the customer experience.[2]

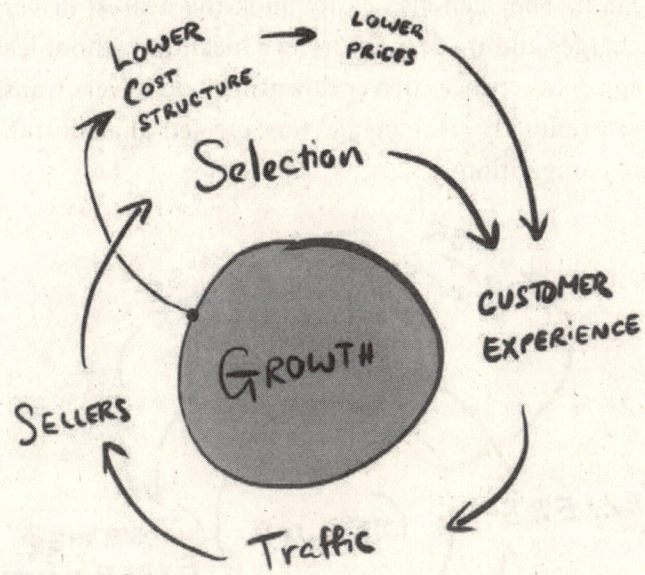

From the above wheel, you learn that Amazon's lower prices result in more customer visits, and with more customer visits, the volume of sales increases. More customers in the platform also encourage commission-paying third-party sellers, allowing the company to get out of fixed costs, such as fulfillment centers and servers required to run the site. All the above tend to reduce the products' prices.

Examining the below diagram, it is evident that Amazon is ruthless in boosting efficiency. Their main focus is to improve productiveness, lower prices, and amplify customer

[2]Original Amazon Sketch: Jeff Bezos (2001)

experience. With such efficiency, the wheel moves faster. For the Uber business strategy, getting more people to use the cab results in more cab drivers joining their ecosystem. In the company's platform, customers enjoy an improved quality of search. They can also easily book the nearest driver, see the charges and track their driver's location without leaving the app. This reduces driver downtime and lowers transport costs; eventually, real magic was created that outran the entire competition.

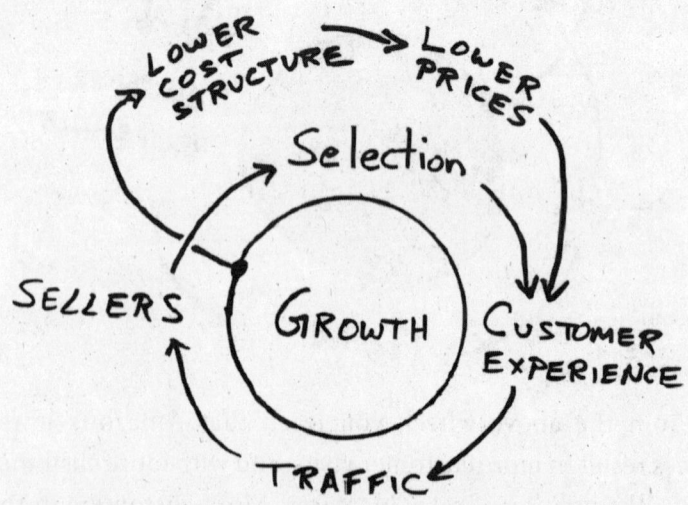

APPLICATION OF THE FLYWHEEL MODEL IN INVESTING

Now that you already understand the flywheel concept and how businesses benefit from it, how can it be implemented in investing? Before starting your investing journey, you should follow the below steps, including examining your mindset, understanding the principles of investing, action-taking, and building investing system. Others include building a portfolio, maintaining investing journal, and reflecting on actions. Finally, we should be improving the thought processes and adding a layer to efficiency. After implementing the first layer, investors should move to the second one, including savings and investing, generating a customized portfolio, risk management, and asset allocation.

STEP 1: LEARNING MINDSET/INVESTMENT PSYCHOLOGY

The first principle when it comes to investing is understanding yourself. Anyone who wants to succeed in the investment journey should be willing to learn. Before embarking on this journey, you should ask yourself, am I an aggressive or conservative investor? What is my risk appetite? Am I a fulltime or parttime investor? Is my family income enough to withstand any losses that might be faced, or is it fragile? Do I have adequate reserve funds that can sustain me if I am unable to generate returns in the next 2-3 years? Am I dependent on a single income, or do I have a diversified income stream? Once you know yourself fully, you can then blend your personality with the right investment strategy. In this case, work on your mindset first. The above, among many other questions, allow investors to blend their investment strategy based on who they are.

Unfortunately, many investors never explore their mindset, and they choose an investing plan blindly. Even though there are many elegant and fancy investing plans out there, you need to know what is the best suit for you. Investment plans are never a "one-size fits all" activity, it is highly personalized, and you should choose whatever fits your investment goals and resources. When making equity investments, you should always know the risks involved and hand-pick the right plan accordingly. Moreover, similar to any other occupation, investing is an occupation that requires professionalism.

When sick, do you take a stethoscope, examine yourself and prescribe medication? Of course, not. Similarly, investing is a full-time profession that requires much expertise. Some people effectively educate themselves in investing, which is good. However, others hire an adviser or invest through a mutual fund or PMS for the equity portfolio. With such a plan, you can manage the remaining 5% and monitor whether it overperforms the advisors. If it does, you can gradually shift capital from MF to your own funds. The take-home from this step is that you should always work on your mindset before investing.

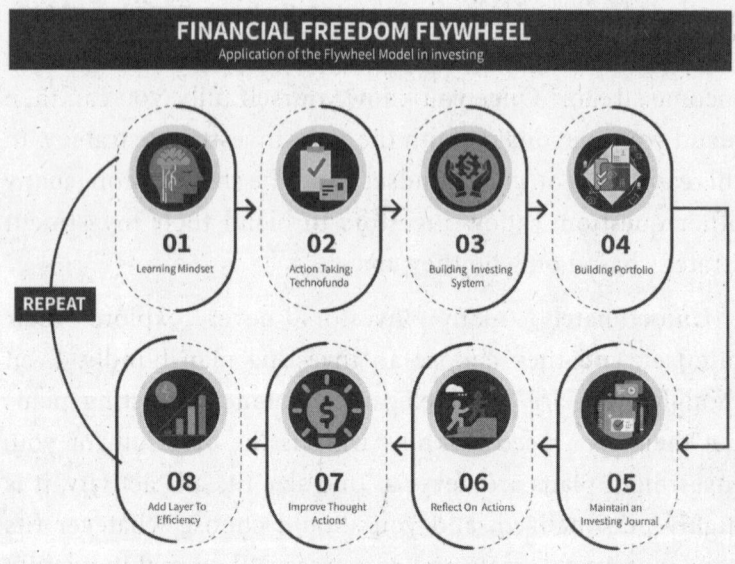

FINANCIAL FREEDOM FLYWHEEL
Application of the Flywheel Model in investing

01 Learning Mindset
02 Action Taking; Technofunda
03 Building Investing System
04 Building Portfolio

REPEAT

08 Add Layer To Efficiency
07 Improve Thought Actions
06 Reflect On Actions
05 Maintain an Investing Journal

STEP 2: ACTION TAKING: TECHNOFUNDA

Knowledge is power, but knowledge without actions becomes useless. Some people spend much time acquiring knowledge that they seldom or never use. When it comes to investing, learning is the first step, but it should be followed with knowledge implementation in the investment framework. Investors should ensure that they understand various compounding principles. Any investor who understands these principles can take advantage of them. These fundamentals have been proven and worked for or against the entire universe over the years. Before investing, you should always have an investment goal/objective. Why am I investing? Some people invest in their children's education, while others invest in buying a house or even a car. Unfortunately, people continue making mistakes when choosing an investment goal. For example, if you want to buy a car after a year, investing in stocks would be a bad idea because of too much fluctuation. Within one or two months, the market can go anywhere.

After selecting the investment goal, the second principle is to understand the compounding effect. Different asset classes tend to compound at different rates. However, the thumb Rule of 72 exists. If you divide the expected rate of return by 72, the quotient is the number of years required to double the money. For example, when you divide 72 by 10, you will require 7.2 years to double the money. For high-growth investing, if 72 is divided by 24, the answer is 3, which means you will need 3 years to double your money. Interestingly, for ₹ 100 growing at 24%, it will become ₹ 200 in 3 years. But after another year, it will be ₹ 800. This is how compounding works. Once you have understood the principles, the next step involves developing a plan related to your asset allocation in various asset classes. It is worth noting that different classes require different competencies. There are two competency options available, which include developing competency towards a particular asset class or outsourcing competency by hiring an investment advisor.

Screening is also the key to making investment choices. With many companies operating in different sectors, one cannot possibly analyze every one of them. Hence, you need to filter companies and eliminate those that fall outside the defined investment criteria. With the ones left, a deeper analysis should be conducted to examine whether they have qualities that match your investment universe and coverage bracket. Thoroughly screen the company you want to invest in through fundamental (relating to company-specific rations, e.g., financial statements) or technical screening (relating to price and volume).

STEP 3: BUILDING INVESTING SYSTEM

As an investor, you need to build an investing system, the entire investing framework. This includes how you will buy various stocks and how to add them and exit when necessary. Without such a framework in place, it becomes challenging to make the grade. Being jumpy from one step to the other is a recipe for failure. Hence, prudent investors go from one step to another, including learning, understanding investing principles, start taking action, and later, start building investing systems. Building an investing system requires the investor to conduct sector, company, and technical analysis.

Investment companies are analyzed through metrics and ratios, and as an investor, you have to choose the sector you want to invest in, e.g., mining, real estate and so on. Before making an investment choice, it is also imperative to conduct company-specific research. This research compares companies with their peers, historical financial statements analysis, forensic accounting, and management quality analysis.

The next analysis is known as technical analysis/PV action. Investors should use both technical and fundamental analysis when choosing a company to invest in. Many investors prefer the fundamental analysis because of past successful histories. However, this analysis has some drawbacks, and one of them is fixated data and numbers. Another limitation of technical analysis is, as it focuses on market psychology, this largely ignores the business's big picture. In this case, a wise investor chooses to blend both the technical and the fundamental analysis.

STEP 4: BUILDING PORTFOLIO

In this step, you should customize a capital allocation portfolio. Capital allocation refers to investing the company's financial resources in a way that increases its effectiveness and maximizes profits. Companies, look forward to investing their resources in a way that generates as much wealth as possible. As an individual investor, an effective portfolio should indicate your wins, losses, and errors. Later, you should analyze the errors and reflect on the next actions. This helps investors to avoid repeating mistakes. For portfolio allocation and rebalancing, a stock market crash results in dislocating the portfolio of high-quality companies. This occurs due to the differential drawdowns in the share prices of constituent stocks. Rebalancing such a portfolio leads to the generation of more returns, and it also sidesteps the risk of being left with uninvested cash. One of the major issues investors face when it comes to rebalancing is the test of conviction of fundamentals of various portfolio companies when undergoing significant drawdowns.

STEP 5: MAINTAIN AN INVESTING JOURNAL

Many people maintain a trading journal but fail to maintain an investment journal. An investing journal is imperative in investing as it shows what is profitable and the residue risk in the system trading, among others.

STEP 6: REFLECT ON ACTIONS

Know what should be maintained and what should be changed. For instance, equity remains one of the most rewarding asset classes. However, it has risks, and hence, it is unwise for an investor to keep all the eggs in one basket, i.e. to put all their savings in an equity market. Therefore, you should diversify your investments across asset classes while ensuring that equity remains a significant portion. What you examine, measure, and analyze are what matter.

STEP 7: IMPROVE THOUGHT PROCESS

If you need to thrive in life and the investing sector, you must be a lifelong learner. There is always the next level to pursue. This is where the right ecosystem where you can connect with like-minded investors becomes very important. Also, in markets, one should not only learn from own mistakes and losses but also from the mistakes of others. I have covered this concept of Vicarious Learning in a later chapter.

STEP 8: ADD LAYER TO EFFICIENCY

The internet remains one of the major sources of information nowadays. With a single mouse click, one can attain an unbelievable amount of data that can assist in making an effective investment decision and help monitor how various investments are performing. As an investor, you should ensure that you get the best resources and tools that can help you easily monitor the progress of your investment while you focus on things that matter. This fetches exponential results. These tools also offer better and faster insights, and they help investors analyze more business and investment frameworks speedingly. For example, investors can use various tools on the internet to gain information.

After the above first layer of the flywheel has been dealt with, another wheel illustrated in the diagram below kicks in. The flywheel's second layer steps include savings and investing, generating portfolio returns, risk management, churning losses/adding winners, and ensuring better capital appreciation. While the first layer focuses on investing, the inside layer focuses on the money element. If an individual learns about his/her mindset, builds an investing system, and even develops an investing journal but fails to learn the principles of personal financing, including a budget, the earlier steps become futile. Therefore, saving and investing alongside this whole system becomes critical. The second step in this second layer is, generating portfolio returns. The investor should examine and test the waters by using real money instead of a paper portfolio. It is advisable to observe the actual portfolio returns rather than the paper one.

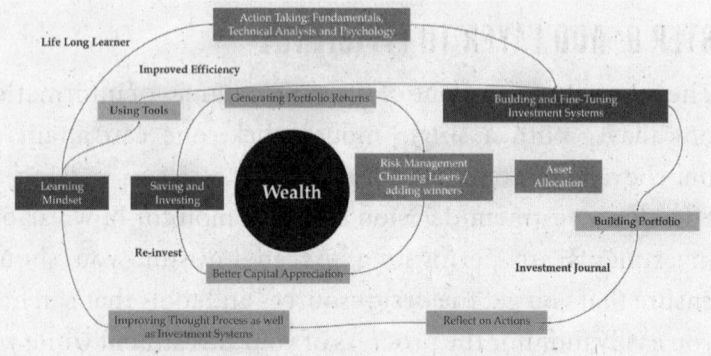

The next step involves asset allocation. Once you realize the losses and churn them, and add wins, you should optimize returns through asset allocation. The link below can help you in sketching out your assets.[3] This is where you can create better capital appreciation and then reinvest both the capital and the returns. You can fabricate a compounding cycle that generates wealth. Once you get the flywheel kicking, you will build wealth and create a magic of financial freedom where you will never have to worry about money. You will become financially *aatmanirbhar* (self-reliant)!

BONUS:

To Learn Building Investing System >>

http://TechnoFunda.co/Live

---

[3]https://technofunda.buzzsprout.com/1667647/8267603-010-powerful-portfolio-allocation-strategies

CHAPTER SUMMARY

- This chapter explores more on TechnoFunda's pillars of investment, which include:

1. MINDSET/INVESTING PSYCHOLOGY

- Before investing, an individual needs to answer a few questions. What is your risk appetite? What kind of investor are you, conservative or aggressive? Are you entering the stock market full-time or part-time (alongside another occupation), among other questions?

- Investing is never a "one size fits all"; hence, one should research and choose what works for them.

- If you plan to make an equity investment, you should thoroughly research it, know the risks involved, and choose the right plan accordingly.

2. PRINCIPLES

- As an investor, always understand the proven universal principles and take advantage of them.

- Have investing objectives and later choose an appropriate asset class.

- As an investor, understand the compound effect. Compounding has different asset compounds; however; the thumb rule is 72.

3. SCREENING

- Thoroughly screen the company you want to invest in either through fundamental (relating to company-specific rations, e.g., financial statements) or technical screening (relating to price and volume).

- After the first screening, conduct a deeper analysis to have a few companies that can be included in the investment and coverage bracket.

4. SECTOR ANALYSIS/COMPANY ANALYSIS

- Investment companies are analyzed through metrics and ratios.

- As an investor, you have to choose the sector you want to invest in, e.g., mining, real estate, etc.

- Before making an investment choice, it is imperative to conduct company-specific research.

5. TECHNICAL ANALYSIS/PV ACTION

- When choosing a company to invest in, investors should use both technical and fundamental analysis.

- Many investors prefer the fundamental analysis because of past successful histories. However, it has one main issue that includes fixated data and numbers.

- Technical analysis also has an issue since it focuses on market psychology and largely ignores the business's big picture.

6. CAPITAL ALLOCATION

- Refers to investing in a firm's financial resources to increase its efficiency and maximize profits. Other key pillars to check include:

7. PORTFOLIO ALLOCATION AND REBRANDING

8. ASSET ALLOCATION

9. TOOLS AND RESOURCES

YOUR REFLECTIONS

(Reflect on what you have learned and pen down your thoughts)

_____

_____

_____

_____

_____

_____

_____

_____

_____

_____

_____

_____

_____

_____

_____

_____

_____

PART 2

IMPLEMENT

CHAPTER THREE

FIRST PRINCIPLES - DRIVERS OF MEGA COMPOUNDING MACHINE

"As to methods, there may be a million and then some, but principles are few. The man who grasps principles can successfully select his own methods. The man who tries methods, ignoring principles, is sure to have trouble."
—Harrington Emerson

When Elon Musk, who has built several multi-billion companies, started the development process of the TESLA car, many experts cautioned him about the high costs that could make those cars unpopular due to inherent battery costs. The battery costs were $600/kw, which were super expensive.

Elon Musk asked - Why $600/kw? And the rest is history. Below is the explanation of how Elon Musk broke this problem with First Principles:

...they would say, "historically, it costs $600 per kilowatt-hour. And so it's not going to be much better than that in the future." ... So the first principle would be ... what are the material constituents of the batteries? What is the spot market value of the material constituents? ... It's got cobalt, nickel, aluminum, carbon, and some polymers for separation, and a steel can.

So break that down on a material basis; if we bought that on a London Metal Exchange, what would each of these things cost? Oh, jeez, it's ... $80 per kilowatt-hour. So, clearly, you just need to think of clever ways to take those materials and combine them into the shape of a battery cell, and you can have batteries that are much, much cheaper than anyone realizes.[1]

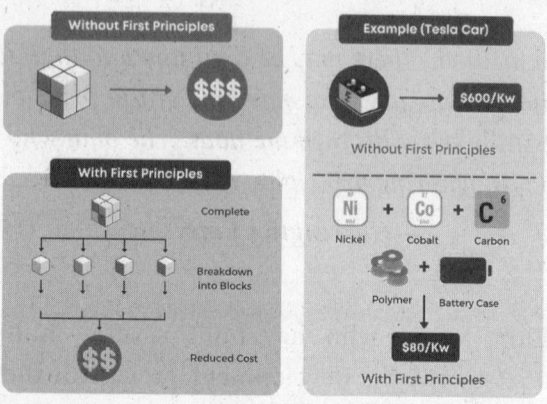

[1]Farnam Street (blog), https://fs.blog/first-principles/

Bottom line: Take a problem, break it down to build blocks by using first-principles, and deep dive into these building blocks. This can help in a logical outcome.

Even billionaire investor Charlie Munger analyses companies from the perspective of first principles to make his investment decision.

The ancient Greek philosopher Aristotle describes how to gain knowledge from basic elements as he defines the first principle as *"the first basis from which a thing is known"*.

First-principles thinking is one of the best ways to reverse-engineer complicated problems and unleash creative possibilities. The idea is to break down complicated problems into basic elements and then reassemble them from the ground up.

It's one of the best ways to learn to think for yourself, unlock your creative potential, and move from linear to non-linear results.[2]

Legendary hedge fund manager Ray Dalio has written, "Principles are fundamental truths that serve as the foundations for behavior that gets you what you want out of life. They can be applied again and again in similar situations to help you achieve your goals. Every day, each of us is faced with a blizzard of situations we must respond to. Without principles we would be forced to react to all the things life throws at us individually, as if we were experiencing each of them for the first time. If instead we classify these situations into types and have good principles for dealing with them, we

---

[2]Farnam Street (blog), https://fs.blog/first-principles/

will make better decisions more quickly and have better lives as a result. Having a good set of principles is like having a good collection of recipes for success. All successful people operate by principles that help them be successful, though what they choose to be successful at varies enormously, so their principles vary."[3]

Let's now apply these first principles to investing.

What are the building blocks of investing returns? It's entry price and exit price. Let's say, you bought a stock at INR 100 and sold it at INR 1000, you will generate 10x capital of your investment. So, remember, the entry price is very important and so is the exit price.

Now, let's break it down further. What are the drivers of entry and exit prices?

1. ***Business Performance***: Let's say, when you bought a stock at INR 100, the earning per share was INR 10. And during the exit, the earning per share was INR 50. This means growth in earning due to business performance contributed 5x returns out of total returns.

2. ***Market Psychology***: Your entry P/E (Price/Earning) multiple was 100/10, i.e. 10x, and when you exited, someone bought from you at P/E multiple of 1000/50, i.e. 20x. Hence, PE re-rating generated the remaining return.

---

[3]Ray Dalio, *Principles: Life and Work* (New York: Simon & Schuster, 2017)

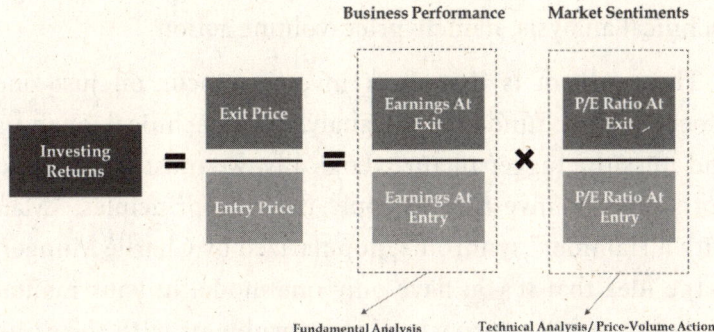

Further breaking it down to first principles…

How can we understand business performance? Through fundamental analysis, namely the 'four cylinders' of sales growth, operating leverage, margin improvement, and debt reduction.

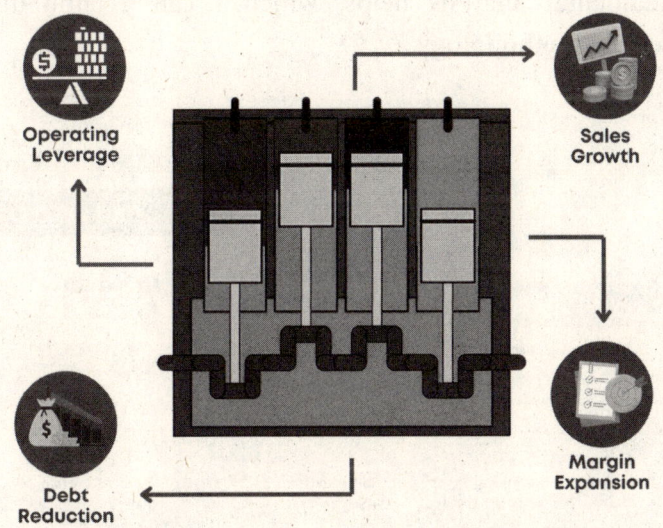

FOUR CYLINDERS THAT FIRE COMPOUNDING MACHINE

And how to understand market psychology? It's through technical analysis, namely price-volume action.

The problem is that most investors focus on just one aspect, either fundamental analysis or technical analysis and miss the bigger picture. Logically, we must understand both sides of investing to apply the first principles. "Man with a Hammer" syndrome, popularized by Charlie Munger, is the idea that if you have only one model in your mental toolkit, you will **approach all your problems with the same solution, even when it may be better to use multiple tools. Either technical or fundamental analysis in isolation is like a single tool; if you only use that one tool for every problem, you will be the metaphorical 'man with a hammer, to whom every problem looks like a nail'.**

This is where blending both technical analysis and fundamental analysis helps, which I call TechnoFunda Investing methodology.

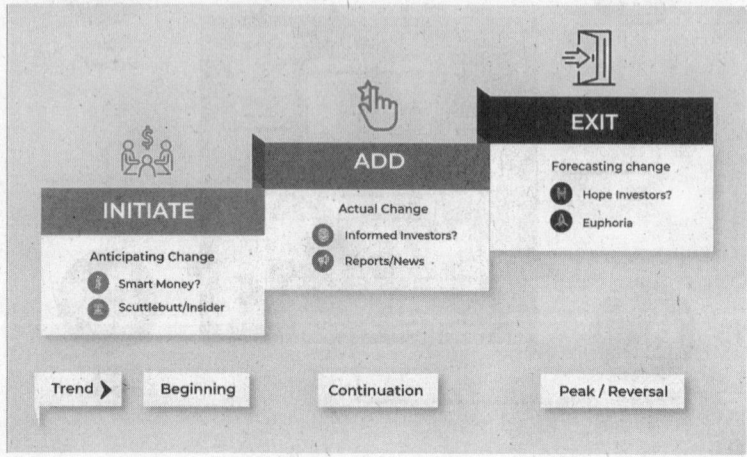

"Value doesn't move stock prices; people do by placing buy orders. Value is only part of the equation. Ultimately you need demand."

—Mark Minervini[4]

'Value' stocks, in isolation, can remain undervalued for long periods. Think of holding companies that always, sustainably, trade at a discount to the cumulative value of their investments (holding company discount). What works is value investing with a 'trigger' to unlock that value. That push is typically a special situation, e.g., a demerger, promoter/management change, etc. Ultimately, when an undervalued stock reverts to intrinsic value, it occurs through price appreciation. Hence, technical analysis can help capture such potential occurrences, while fundamental analysis will confirm it.

Howard Marks shared the importance of understanding market psychology in his book *The Most Important Thing*, "Would-be investors can take courses in finance and accounting, read widely and, if they are fortunate, receive mentoring from someone with a deep understanding of the investment process. But only a few of them will achieve superior insight, intuition, sense of value and awareness of psychology required for consistently getting above-average results."[5]

You can't do the same things as other investors do and get an edge. While most investors follow only one aspect, you can

---

[4]Mark Minervini, *Trade like a stock market wizard* (New York: McGraw Hill, 2013)

[5]Howard Marks, *The Most Important Thing* (New York: Columbia University Press, 2011)

master the art by understanding both business performance and market psychology. Essentially, price movements are the collective buy and sell transactions of the market and, hence, price-volume action is a crucial insight into investors' psychology.

Let's now dive deeper into price-volume action. This is something that investors rarely practice or shy away with. It helps us make better decisions around screening and is an early warning indicator for our investing decisions - whether to buy, add or sell.

Chatur, while resting his chin over his knuckles, "If there is so much fundamental information available out there in terms of books, research reports, conference calls, industry reports, etc., then why do I need to do the hard work to understand all this?"

Aryan beamed his cheek-to-cheek smile and replied, "Well, the answer to this will unfold slowly as we delve into this subject."

THE CONTEXT

Now, let's put our thinking hats ON and reckon what happens on a normal day in the stock market? Of course - we all know >> buying and selling of securities.

Further digging deeper, each transaction leaves its footprints and there are decisions from investors/traders/speculators that have caused that transaction. And for every transaction, there are two facets - quantity and price at which the transaction has happened.

This tells us that PRICE and VOLUME are two fundamental building blocks of all the transactions that happen on the stock market. And most importantly, they leave a footprint on transactions of all market participants and, indirectly, their behavior and decision points.

An interesting point is that all the technical indicators are second-order derivatives of these two basic building blocks with certain mathematical formulas applied around them. Think of RSI, Moving Averages, ADX, etc. As in physics, so in statistics: the output cannot be more precise, in terms of the number of significant figures, than the inputs. The same applies to price volume action: indicators derived from price and volume cannot be more precise than price and volume themselves.

So, it gives a tremendous advantage logically, if we can capture price-volume action firsthand and can infer the actions of market participants to an extent. It can work as an early warning indicator. Hence, we should never ignore price-volume action.

The next question that might surface in your mind is how to capture these footprints, how to apply and how to make the best use of them?

Well, it depends upon our creativity and depth of fundamental implications of various actions and we can back-calculate such parameters from price-volume action to our advantage.

Let me give a few simple examples:

(a) We know there are price-volume breakouts when some fundamental news about the company excites the market participants - say CapEx announcement, above expected results, any approvals, new product announcement, tax sops for the sector, etc. Most time, these things happen even before the news is out.

A simple way to capture these mathematically is by putting screens like - Today price increase >4% and volume > 2x the 1-week-average.

(b) Say there is sector news that moves all the sector participants due to positive happenings in the sector. When stocks of the whole sector rise, it is a powerful signal.[6]

Business Standard ⋮

Policy tailwinds to drive 15% CAGR in defence production

India News · Economics · Social Sciences

14 Nov 2023   +5 more   AJAI SHUKLA

Amidst rising defence spending by East European and West Asian countries, a new report from Axis Capital Research focuses on India's defence production and indigenisa–

You can capture these by building screens mapped by sector to get a glimpse of such price fluctuations.

These are powerful tools.

---

[6]Business Standard

Sector Community Pulse

Nov 09 2023

SECTOR	FAV.	TOTAL COMPANIES	09 NOV	08 NOV	07 NOV	06 NOV	03 NOV	02 NOV	01 NOV
Auto - 2W	☆	4	100	50	50	50	25	0	50
Auto - PV/Trucks	☆	4	75	25	0	0	25	50	25
Defense - Ship Building	☆	3	66	33	33	0	0	0	0
Infra - Laminates	☆	9	55	55	33	33	66	22	11

Home > Market Pulse > Defense - Ship Building (all)

COMPANY NAME	SECTOR	MARKET CAP	SYMBOL	ISIN	WEIGHTED RPI	52WK HIGH W.RPI	LATEST PRICE	52WK HIGH
Cochinship	Defense - Ship Building	Small Cap	COCHINSHIP	INE704P01017	140.55		1037.60	
Grse	Defense - Ship Building	Small Cap	GRSE	INE382Z01011	119.02		779.40	
Mazagon dock	Defense - Ship Building	Mid Cap	MAZDOCK	INE249Z01012	143.21		1996.45	

Now let's understand what drives earnings growth and business performance.

The essence of fundamental analysis can be summarized in terms of four cylinders. These are the four main catalysts and all the aspects of fundamental research can be categorized under one of these four. You will also notice that all the questions asked by analysts and investors in conference calls revolve around these Four Points.

Below are the four-cylinders that fire compounding MACHINE:

1. Sales growth,
2. Operating leverage,
3. Margin expansion and
4. Debt reduction

Another important aspect to understand besides earnings growth is the quality of business, mostly captured by the return on capital employed. We will learn more about this through the TREES analogy in subsequent chapters.

Beady-eyed Chatur: I am enthused to know more about this analogy, but before we forge ahead, can you recommend some visual way to retain this knowledge about technicals and fundamentals?

Aryan: Of course, Chatur, **if you are interested in learning through audio-visual format, you can watch my video at:**

https://www.youtube.com/watch?v=umkUDnHjXM4

Traders Carnival 2018: How to Blend Technicals and Fundamentals by Vivek Mashrani, CFA

CHAPTER SUMMARY

- Investment principles are few compared to methods, and when one understands principles, method selection becomes easy.

- To maximize profits as well as reduce inputs, businesses should incorporate the first principles.

- First-principles include taking the challenge (the problem), breaking it into building blocks using principles that assist in the logical outcomes, and later deep-diving into building blocks.

- First-principles thinking is one of how people reverse engineer-complicated issues and unleash creative possibilities. E.g., breaking down complicated issues and later assembling them from the ground up.

- First-principles thinking is a great way to learn to think by oneself, unlock creative potential, and move from linear to nonlinear results.

- An example of an individual who used the first principles is Elon Musk. When he began developing the TESLA car, he was warned of the high cost of batteries ($600/Kw). Using the first principle, he broke down the materials used to shape the battery cell. Later, he realized that by buying the materials from London Metal Exchange, the costs would come down from $600/Kw to $80/Kw hence profit maximization.

- What are the first principles of investing? What are the building blocks of investing returns? The answer is the entry and exit price. For example, with a stock of

100, one can make 1000, which means 10x capital of the investment. The business drivers for both entry and exit prices include:

- **Business performance**- analyzed through fundamental analysis that involves sales growth, operating leverage, margin improvement, and debt reduction

- **Market psychology**- analyzed through technical analysis, also known as price-volume action

YOUR REFLECTIONS

(Reflect on what you have learned and pen down your thoughts)

_____

_____

_____

_____

_____

_____

_____

_____

_____

_____

_____

_____

_____

_____

_____

_____

_____

CHAPTER FOUR

SCREENING FOR MEGA-COMPOUNDERS

"Simplicity results from long, hard work, not the starting point. The ability to reduce something to its essence is the true mark of understanding. But one of the greatest ironies in life is that when the smartest minds generously share the secrets of their success with us, we ignore them, because they sound too basic and simple for us to appreciate."[1]

I have tried to simplify mega compounding into a simple Tree analogy so it is easier to understand. It took me a long time to come to the essence of the entire business selection framework. Let's now scuba-dive into this.

The first step of mega compounding is to look for great businesses rather than mediocre ones. This is when the

---

[1]Gautam Baid, *The Joys of Compounding* (New York, Columbia University Press, 2020)

compounding of capital will be intrinsic, i.e. within the business. As per the first principles, the bulk of the returns is directly proportionate to the business performance. In the TechnoFunda construct, this is categorized as the core portfolio. Ideally, this comprises 70% of an investor's equity allocation.

We will use two parameters to classify businesses: return on capital employed and earnings growth. Using these two metrics, we can arrive at a 2x2 grid.

RoCE - Return on Capital Employed

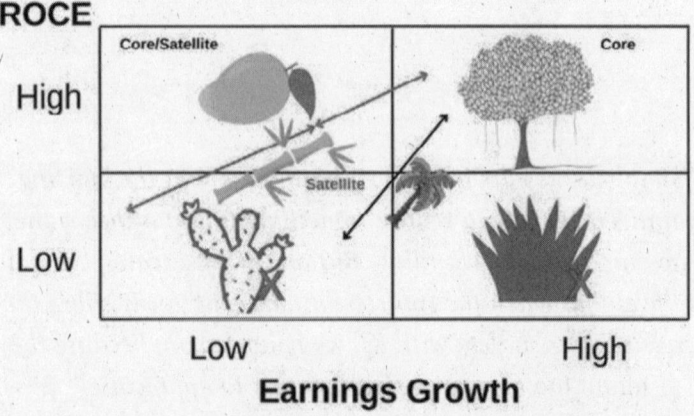

The top right quadrant, which is a high return on capital employed and high earnings growth, is what we call the Banyan Tree. This bucket is the holy grail of long-term investing. If you can find even one or two Banyan Trees in your lifetime, you will be very rich.

High RoCE but low earnings growth is like a Mango Tree. This depicts companies that cannot reinvest capital at high rates of return. Thus, they distribute profits to shareholders in dividends, which we have equated to the mango fruit. You can finance your lifestyle with these dividends, equivalent to enjoying aamras or aamrakhand (mango juice).

Low RoCE but high earnings growth is a weed. It grows rapidly but consumes the nutrients and water required for the Banyan Trees in your portfolio.

Low RoCE with low earnings growth is a cactus- full of thorns, and it is often obvious for the investors to stay away from these. Let us learn the nuts and bolts of each of these.

Also, we have Bamboo Trees, which are on the path to improvement and Palm Trees, which are primarily cyclical companies transitioning very fast between low to high and vice versa.

Banyan Trees: These are companies whose operating profit is going back to the fixed asset to create new capacities and generate growth. This is where there is intrinsic compounding within the business. These businesses are consistent compounders. They have longevity, sustainability and consistency. Often, such companies are well-known among the market participants and are thus richly priced, which is well-deserved. You can reap the reward by investing in these companies after detailed research into the company's source of competitive advantage. You can compute the market factors in the next 3 to 5 years of earnings in such businesses through a reverse DCF (Discounted Cash Flow). DCF is a technique used to estimate the value of an investment depending on its future cash flows.

Here's the formula to calculate DCF:

$$DCF = CF_t/(1+r)^t$$

CF_t = cash flow in period t

R = Appropriate discount rate that has given the riskiness of the cash flows

t = life of the asset, which is valued

Being an investor, you can gain an edge by a) understanding whether growth in cash flows will outpace growth in net profit (e.g. by working capital cycle reduction) b) having a time horizon of greater than 5 years, as the market can very rarely discount beyond this. In such Banyan Tree companies, the correction from the peak valuation is limited. They optically appear to be expensive at the time of buying, but in hindsight, they almost always are undervalued due to the unexpected longevity and magnitude of growth. With a broader market crash, an investor may find the valuations of these Banyan Tree companies attractive - buying them is usually a wise choice. Stock price follows the earnings growth and a lollapalooza effect (coined by Charlie Munger – it means a confluence of factors acting together can be especially powerful drivers of human behavior and this can lead to both positive and negative results) occurs. Banyan Tree companies show superb capital efficiency and outstanding growth of earnings. It is fertile territory for finding multi-year compounding machines and yet offers great safety during tough market conditions. These are the Enduring multi-baggers.

Mango Trees: What is the USP of a mango tree? It keeps giving you juicy, sweet fruits. It gives all the cash flow in dividends or buybacks. These are the blue-chip companies that dividend investors often hold in their portfolios. However, if all the cash flow generated by a firm with a high RoCE is returned to shareholders, then it is difficult for the firm to grow its revenues over time. These are usually the large and aging companies expected to grow slightly faster than the economy. Such companies started as fast-growers and eventually drifted to becoming slow-growers. When an industry, at large, slows down, most companies within the industry lose momentum.

For example, penetration in the toothpaste market has increased dramatically, therefore, there is little room for further expansion in this industry. Hence the growth rate of Colgate has decreased significantly and it has become a Mango Tree company. The quality of Mango Tree companies is unquestionable, but an investor should know the possible growth rates. An expectation of generating 20 to 25% of returns through these is imprudent. The right way to look at these is not from the lens of capital appreciation but capital preservation. An example could be ITC. The stock chart of a Mango Tree company over 4-5 years, is typically flat or there is a very slight increase. The steepness of the slope is very small. Peter Lynch writes- "Another sure sign of a slow grower is that it pays a generous and regular dividend ... companies pay generous dividends when they can't dream up new ways to use the money to expand the business."[2] Such mango companies may prove to be Quality Traps. The high quality of these companies blinds the investors to the possibility that these companies may not be able to grow their earnings at a healthy pace due to low underlying base rates, e.g., Colgate. As a result, stock performance remains disappointing.

Cactus: What are the characteristics of a cactus? How does cactus operate? It does not grow too much or too fast (low earnings growth), and it has sharp thorns (returns below the cost of capital). But it doesn't consume too much water either! It is very conservative in its intake of water. These are low RoCE businesses that do not grow much. Due to its visible numerical economic characteristics, just like the sharp thorns of a cactus, investors know they must avoid them. The only good part about these businesses is that they generally don't re-invest cash flow for growth and mostly pay it as dividends or buybacks.

---

[2]Peter Lynch, *One Up On Wall Street*, (New York: Simon & Schuster, 1989)

Typically, these businesses trade below book value and low price-earnings ratio for obvious reasons of low growth and low RoCE. There could also be a high dividend yield if management is distributing cash flows to shareholders.

Often those who poorly understand businesses can get lured by low valuation and/or the high dividend yield, only to eventually realize these were value traps. They think they are doing "value investing", but they aren't applying the principles of value investing properly.

Warren Buffett has beautifully explained the true meaning of value investing in his 1992 Annual Letter to Shareholders:

"Whether appropriate or not, the term "value investing" is widely used. Typically, it connotes the purchase of stocks having attributes such as a low ratio of price to book value, a low price-earnings ratio, or a high dividend yield. Unfortunately, such characteristics, even if they appear in combination, are far from determinative as to whether an investor is buying something for what it is worth, and is therefore operating on the principle of obtaining value in his investments. Correspondingly, opposite characteristics—*a high ratio of price to book value, a high price-earnings ratio, and a low dividend yield—are in no way inconsistent with a "value" purchase [emphasis added]."*[3]

Weeds: They suck enormous amounts of water and will not allow a good flower to grow. Such investments will just grow for the sake of growth, but these are low RoCE businesses, so the more they grow, the more they destroy value. They spoil the growth for the remaining part of your garden. Therefore, they just suck out the resources, but don't give optimal RoCE. These are the businesses earning 6% RoCE and you keep growing and keep putting capital again and again. It is like a bottomless pit of capital. Or we can say, it is like pouring petrol into a tank which is hollow, and all the oil goes down the drain- but you keep pouring it! Often, market participants, including institutional investors blindly chase growth. They fail to understand that in a low RoCE business, low growth is better than high growth! When RoCE is high, growth creates value; if not, growth destroys it! If a company's RoCE remains below the Cost of Capital for long, then high growth decreases value. So, the company must raise significant levels of capital from its equity holders to fund its growth. If a company's RoCE is equal to its Cost of Capital, then no amount of growth adds any value. Growth adds positive value only when RoCE is higher than the Cost of Capital. This is counterintuitive for most investors, but it is a crucial principle. Such companies may prove to be Growth Traps. High growth in these companies is most likely due to cyclical upturns but gets mistaken for secular high growth.

---

[3]Warren Buffett, *Berkshire Hathaway 1992 Annual Letter to Shareholders*, March 1, 1993 http://www.berkshirehathaway.com/letters/1992.html

Such stocks may still end up as multi-baggers, but at best, transitory multi-baggers. Therefore, it is very important to have exit criteria because not exiting can lead to 'giving back' all your previous gains to the market.

As Warren Buffett wrote in his letter in 2007:

"The worst sort of business is one that grows rapidly, requires significant capital to engender the growth, and then earns little or no money. Think airlines. Here a durable competitive advantage has proven elusive ever since the days of the Wright Brothers…"

Further, he wrote in 1983:

"…as they generally earn low rates of return – rates that often barely provide enough capital to fund the inflationary needs of the existing business, with nothing left over for real growth, for distribution to owners, or for the acquisition of new businesses…"

Bamboo: Bamboo Trees are the ones that are not cyclical but potentially, they have low growth and/or low RoCE. There are certain triggers that manifest and finally, it does exponential growth along with high RoCE (just like bamboo, which remains below the ground for initial few years and then shoots up).

Again, whether they will stay there as Banyan or Mango or come back to Cactus is not known in advance. Therefore, we need to continuously monitor and allocate gradually to these businesses, as this can give multi-fold returns if we ride them correctly. Eventually, if they become consistent compounders, i.e., Banyan Tree, they give super-normal returns through re-rating as well. So, there is a dual benefit here: exponential growth coupled with high RoCE and the possibility of re-rating if they perform as expected. Turnaround scenarios can fall under this category.

Palm: This is a typical short cycle - what is popularly known as cyclical stocks. Their sales and profits rise and fall frequently. It can include companies in sectors like paper, sugar, steel, etc. These companies transition between low RoCE and low growth to high RoCE and high growth. The key differentiating factor between Bamboo and Palm is that Bamboo has a small probability to become Mango or Banyan, but Palm will always come back to its roots. Entry and exits are very important for taking positions in this category of business.

Palm businesses are the most misunderstood of all types of businesses. Most investors get excited at the peak of the cycle where earnings are at their peak. The PE ratio might optically look cheap/low and stories float around that these earnings are to stay and businesses are undergoing structural change. This is a perfect recipe for disaster most of the time.

For further elaboration on whether all growth is good, let us hear from Terry Smith. "In our view, growth cannot be thought about sensibly in isolation from returns. Rapid growth may be good news or it may be bad news. It depends on how much capital you must invest to generate that growth. The "earnings" of a bank savings account will grow faster, the more money you deposit into the account. But it is unlikely to be a good investment strategy to put most of your assets into such an account, and you certainly shouldn't rejoice at the fact that if you double your capital invested, you will get twice as much interest. That is not growth. The source of growth is also a factor to consider. Growth in profits from increasing prices can simply build an umbrella beneath which competitors can flourish. We are more interested in companies which have a physical growth in the merchandise or service sold than simple pricing power, although that's nice too."[4]

It is very important to make a distinction between Mango and Banyan. Banyans can re-invest either organically (e.g., by setting up a new factory) or inorganically (e.g., by acquiring other companies). As Chuck Akre says, "If a business has a high return on owner's capital, we would like them to be able to take all the free cash they generate and put it back into that business to continue to earn those high rates of return. It's way more efficient than paying us a dividend."[5]

The biggest paradox in long-term investing is choosing between Cactus and Weeds. Most investors prefer Weeds over Cactus, as at least there is a growth in earnings. However, Cactus is often better than Weeds. Because Cactus has distinctly visible thorns, it is often obvious to avoid them. However, Weeds do not have such explicitly available warning signs.

Often an investor in Mango Tree companies will make small profits, an investor in Banyan Tree companies will make large profits, buying Weed companies will cause large losses and an investor in Cactus companies will only suffer small losses. If you can just avoid Weeds, that is large losses, you will do very well as an equity investor.

---

[4] https://www.fundsmith.co.uk/media/mv3abv1h/owner-s-manual.pdf#page=10
[5] https://economictimes.indiatimes.com/markets/stocks/news/akres-three-legged-stool-theory-to-spot-good-businesses-to-invest-in/articleshow/76659443.cms?from=mdr

Types	Risk vs. Reward	Base Rate
	Low	High
	Low	High
	High	Low
	High	Low

Chatur: I am impressed by this analogy of yours. I strongly recommend that you get it patented. Here's another question for you: Now that I know I must look for Banyan Trees, the question is, how can I find them?

Aryan: This is a million-dollar question. Well, nobody will come and tell you this is a Banyan Tree company. You must do the research and the analysis. We will understand further in the coming chapters how to do this research, but the first principle is to narrow down the number of companies to research. This is done through screening. A website like screener.in is a boon for investors; you can create customized screens based on your preferred criteria.

Palm and Bamboo Trees are mean-reverting; Banyan Trees are upwards trending; and Weeds and Cactus are downwards trending

Mean reverting	• Cyclical sectors like metals, agro, sugar, tea etc.
Trending upwards	• Compounders which has long term upward trend
Trending downwards	• Junk stocks like Suzlon, JP associates, Unitech etc.

For banyans, the highs can be much higher than you can ever imagine!

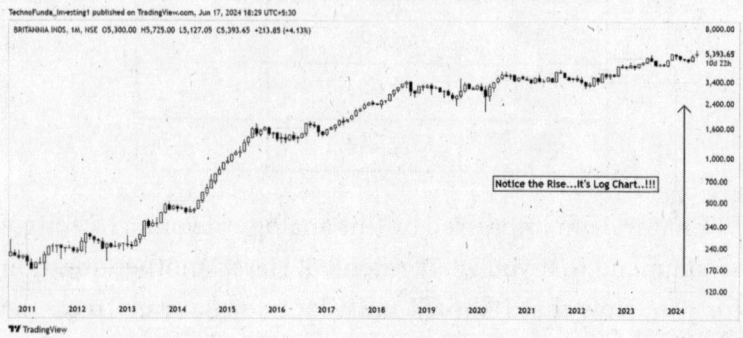

The interesting aspect of the stock market is that often the categorizations of businesses are not stagnant. Banyan Trees are seldom Banyan Trees forever, and so are other categories. Peter Lynch aptly writes, "Companies don't stay in the same category forever. Over my years of watching stocks, I've seen hundreds of them start out fitting one description and end up fitting another."[6]

When Banyan Trees transition into Mango Trees, i.e., quality remains intact, but growth rates slow down, this is often referred to as quality traps in the investing parlance. Often these businesses suddenly face technological disruption and terminal value might go for a toss unless they re-invent. The P/E multiple contracts significantly during such phases, which may lead to long periods of underperformance for the stock. It could be in time-wise correction or a sudden decline

---

[6]Peter Lynch, *One Up On Wall Street* (New York: Simon & Schuster, 1989)

in stock price. Most importantly, because of the wisdom of crowds, this happens *before* actual earnings deceleration is visible in financials. Thus, an investor restricting oneself to fundamentals and ignoring price movements is likely to hold on in such scenarios. This is one of the major risks when investing in Banyan Trees. Therefore, investors in such companies should always be on the lookout for signs of slowing earnings growth. One needs to have an exit strategy in place if it is structural. The worst mistake to make is to buy them thinking that growth might come back without understanding business transition.

"The traditional "value investor" mentality of buying cheap securities, waiting for them to bounce back to "intrinsic value," selling and moving onto the next opportunity, is flawed.

In today's world of instant information and fast-paced innovation, cheap securities increasingly appear to be value traps; often they are companies ailing from technological disruption and long-term decline. This rapid recycling of capital also creates an enormous drag on our after-tax returns. In addition, by focusing on these opportunities, we incur enormous opportunity costs by not focusing instead on the tremendous opportunities created by the exceptional innovation S-curves we are currently witnessing."

—Marcelo Lima

On the positive side, usually, Cactus transitions into Mango Trees or Mango transitions into Banyan Trees. This often occurs in small and Mid-Cap companies and occasionally in commodity and cyclical businesses. This aspect is played in the techno-funda approach through the satellite portfolio, which we will cover in the next chapter.

The table below captures the market condition vs. likely screen outcome.

	Screen Description	Likely outcome	
		Bear Market	Bull Market
Fundamentals	**Classic value screens** • RoE > 20%; RoCE > 20% • P/E < 15x; P/B < 2x • 3 year Sales CAGR > 15-20% • 3 year PAT CAGR > 15-20% • Market Cap/FCF < 10x	Quality Companies Cheap Price Good Compounders	Mostly Junks Contrarian Sectors Value Traps
Technicals	**Tactical screens** • Price-volume breakouts • Volume spurts • New 52 week highs • Sectoral price-volume action • Sudden momentum	Mixed Results Quality Companies Emerging Sectors	Turnarounds Cyclical Sectors Momentum Stocks Structural Changes

Your task for this chapter is to identify one Banyan Tree and one Mango Tree, and email the names of these companies to me at *connect@vivekmashrani.com* (**I will send you special return gift**)

CHAPTER BONUS:

Download Powerful Excel Screener >>

http://TechnoFunda.co/excel

CHAPTER SUMMARY

- When trying to mega compound, the first step should be to search for a big business rather than the mediocre one. Such compounding of capital is intrinsic, i.e., within the business. Refer to the earnings and earnings growth portfolio:

  - High RoCE companies- companies unable to reinvest capital at high rates of return. They distribute profits to shareholders in terms of dividends

  - Low RoCE- grows rapidly but may affect Banyan trees' growth, evident in the portfolio. Low RoCE does not attract investors as a result of low earning growth

BANYAN TREES (REFER TO EARNINGS AND EARNINGS GROWTH)

- Banyan trees refer to companies where operating cost goes back to a fixed asset. Such creates new capacities and generates growth

- Involves intrinsic compounding within the business

- Consistent compounders. Have longevity, consistency, and sustainability

- Well-known among market participants (highly-priced)

- Investors in this group can edge through detailed research of the company's competitive advantage source

- Show superb capital efficiency and outstanding earnings growth; fertile territory for finding multi-year compounding machines
- Offer great safety during tough market conditions. These are enduring multi-baggers.

MANGO TREES

- Gives all the cash flow in the form of dividends or buybacks, making it challenging for them to grow their revenues
- Blue-chip companies that dividend investors hold in their portfolios
- Mostly large and growing companies are expected to grow faster compared to the economy
- They start as fast growers, then slow down. When an industry slowdown, companies under it follow. With an increased toothpaste penetration, there was little room for further expansion of toothpaste through penetration. Hence, Colgate's growth rate decreased

CACTUS

- Has a low earning growth and returns below the cost of capital
- As a result of their visible numerical economic characteristics, investors tend to avoid them
- They do not reinvest cash flow for growth (pay it as dividend or buyback)

- The businesses trade below book value and low price-earnings ratio as a result of low growth as well as low RoCE

- When management distributes cashflows to shareholders, the cactus business can have a high dividend yield

WEEDS

- Low RoCE which grows for the sake of growth

- The more they grow, the more they destroy value

- They earn approximately 6% RoCE, but people continue putting capital on them (bottomless pit of capital)

- When a company's RoCE remains high, growth creates value. If not, growth destroys value. When it's below the Cost of Capital, then high growth decreases value since the company has to raise significant levels of capital from its equity holders to fund its growth. When it's equal to the Cost of Capital, no amount of growth adds any value

BAMBOO

- Not cyclical, but had low growth/low RoCE. However, various triggers activate them to manifest exponential growth

- They need constant monitoring to check whether they will behave as Cactus, Mango, or Banyan

PALM

- Have a short cycle known as cyclical stocks, e.g., sugar, steel, and paper companies

- Sales and profit may rise and fall within a short period

- Represent a transition between Low RoCE and low growth to high RoCE and high growth

- Palm difference from bamboo is that bamboo has a probability of becoming mango or banyan, but the palm always comes back to the roots

- They are mostly misunderstood since investors get excited at the cycle's peak. When earnings are at their peak, the PE ratio might look cheap/low, and stories floating around that these earnings are to stay and that businesses are undergoing structural change

YOUR REFLECTIONS

(Reflect on what you have learned and pen down your thoughts)

_____

_____

_____

_____

_____

_____

_____

_____

_____

_____

_____

_____

_____

_____

_____

_____

_____

_____

_____

CHAPTER FIVE

EVERYTHING IS CYCLICAL

"The more time I spend in the world of investing, the more I appreciate the underlying cyclicity of things."[1]

"Mechanical things can go in a straight line. Time moves ahead continuously. So can a machine when it's adequately powered. But processes in fields like history and economics involve people, and when people are involved, the results are variable and cyclical."

—Howard Marks[2]

Howard Mark in his book *The Most Important Thing* writes:

---

[1]Howard Marks, *The Most Important Thing* (New York: Columbia University Press, 2011)
[2]https://www.nasdaq.com/articles/few-thoughts-about-investing-cyclicals-2016-01-25

"Very few things move in a straight line. There's progress and there's deterioration. Things go well for a while and then poorly. Progress may be swift and then slow down. Deterioration may creep up gradually and then turn climactic. But the underlying principle is that things will wax and wane, grow and decline. The same is true for economics, markets and companies: they rise and fall."

As stated in a previous chapter, psychology is very important. Particularly, in economic activities where humans are involved, we will see cyclicity.

Therefore, we must respect the cyclical nature of life. And when we are aware of <u>where we stand in the cycle</u>, we can make better decisions.

The efficient market hypothesis assumes that investors always act rationally and stocks always trade at their fair market value. However, this is a flawed theory, as the psychology of investors causes them to overreact or underreact in the same situation. This causes cyclicity of undervaluation and overvaluation.

"The market is a pendulum that forever swings between unsustainable optimism & unjustified pessimism. An intelligent investor is a realist who sells to optimists and buys from pessimists."
—Benjamin Graham, The Intelligent Investor

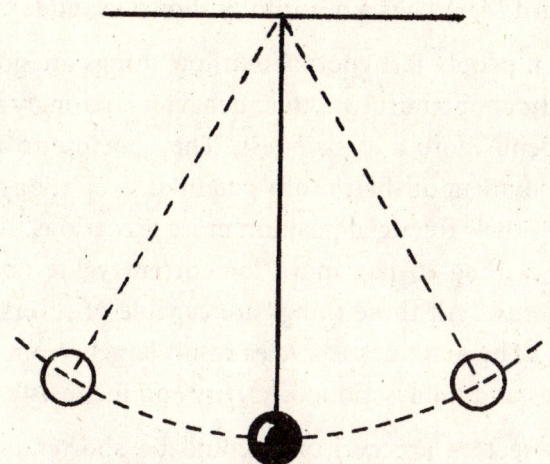

The Market Pendulum moving between
optimism and pessimism

To understand this better, we should first get to the bottoms of the mental model called FEEDBACK LOOPS.

"Every action creates an equal and opposite reaction. When reactions loop back to affect themselves, a feedback loop is created. All real-world systems are composed of many such interacting feedback loops — animals, machines, businesses, and ecosystems, to name a few. There are two types of feedback loops: positive and negative. Positive feedback amplifies system output, resulting in growth or decline. Negative feedback dampers output, stabilizes the system around an equilibrium point."[3]

---

[3]*Universal Principles of Design* by <u>William Lidwell</u>, <u>Kritina Holden</u>, <u>Jill Butler</u> Rockport Publishers, 01-Jan-2010

Howard Marks has a beautifully shown example.[4]

"When people feel good about how things are going and optimistic about the future, their behavior is strongly affected. They spend more and save less. They borrow to increase their enjoyment or their profit potential, even though doing so makes their financial position more precarious. And they become willing to pay more for current value or a piece of the future. All these things are capable of reversing in a second...The extremes of cycles result largely from people's emotions and foibles, nonobjectivity and inconsistency."

Most sectors are cyclical - could be shorter or longer cycles, but it's everywhere. Edward Chancellor has explained this very effectively in his book Capital Returns.

"Initially, investors are optimistic and they put capital in a particular sector/business attracted by the prospect of high returns. This results in competition and returns fall. Eventually, returns fall below the cost of capital and there is industry consolidation and exits. New players are not interested in investing capital. Again, due to lesser supply, returns rise above the cost of capital making - existing players enjoy good returns and make it lucrative for new prospects to enter the industry. This keeps repeating.

It's the game of demand and supply that causes cycles everywhere - be it economy, sectors or businesses."[5]

---

[4]Howard Marks, *The Most Important Thing* (New York: Columbia University Press, 2011)
[5]Edward Chancellor, *Capital Returns* (Basingstoke: Palgrave Macmillan, 2016)

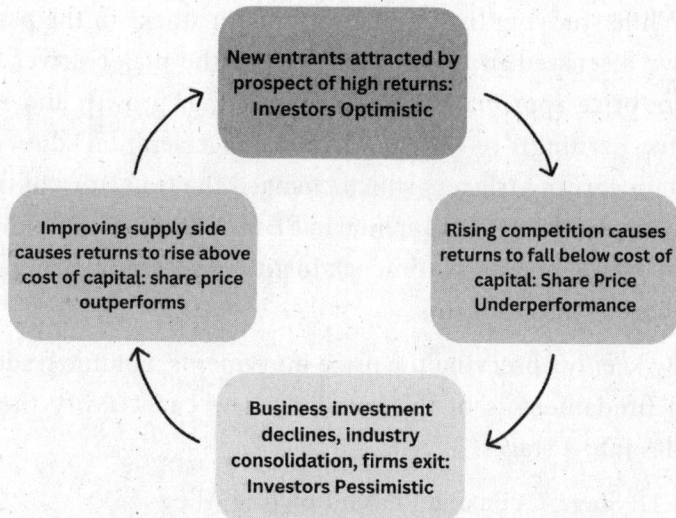

The best part is that the cycle keeps repeating. The more understanding we develop around these patterns and cycles, the more likely we are to benefit from them when they repeat in the future.

There is a powerful mechanism called STAGE ANALYSIS which can be used to understand these cycles. This has been used, popularized and shared by many prominent traders/investors, including Richard Wyckoff, Stan Weinstein, Mark Minervini, etc. I have adopted this concept to blend with fundamental analysis and use it with my framework.

While studying the number of growth stocks in the past, as we discussed in the first principles, the major driver of share price appreciation has been earnings growth and PE (Price-Earning) re-rating. Earnings acceleration due to certain earning triggers which changed the trajectory of the business has been instrumental in PE re-rating (or sometimes even overall market sentiment). Institutional buying has also been one reason for this.

By keenly observing the price movements, volume traded and fundamentals of the company, one can classify these cycles into 4 stages:

1. Stage 1 - Basing Phase: Bowling Alley
2. Stage 2 - Accumulation Phase: Mega Compounding
3. Stage 3 - Distribution Phase: Main Street
4. Stage 4 - Declining Phase: Laggards

Some of these terminologies have been inspired by Geoffrey Moore's book *Crossing the Chasm*. (Harper Business; 3rd edition)

Volume traded and fundamentals of the company, one can generally classify these cycles into 4 stages

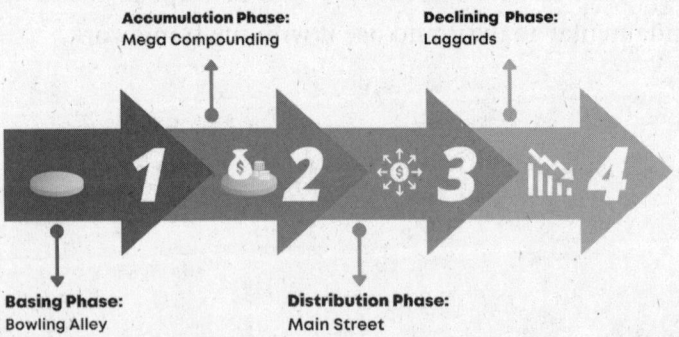

Accumulation Phase:
Mega Compounding

Declining Phase:
Laggards

Basing Phase:
Bowling Alley

Distribution Phase:
Main Street

STAGE 1 - BASE PHASE: BOWLING ALLEY

This is the phase of equilibrium. There are mainly 3 cases when this happens:

1. When a business has low growth with no incremental growth triggers

2. When a business is working on future growth triggers but the execution is uncertain

3. When the overall market condition is lackluster

Bottom line: There is hardly any buying interest. Business is yet to prove its future earnings potential. Stage 1 usually occurs after a fall in prices and looks like a consolidation period.

CHARACTERISTICS OF STAGE 1:

- Overall buying and selling activity will be sluggish

- Price movement is in equilibrium with relatively much lower volumes as bulls and bears are in equilibrium

- The ratio of up days to down days is equal

- There is no trend, and the stock keeps consolidating

- The stock price is below key moving averages

- The average volume on up days is almost equal to the average volume on down days

UNDERLYING REASONS FOR THIS:

- Market participants are in no hurry to buy, waiting for earnings growth triggers

- Due to lack of any institutional buying interest

- Even if potential earnings triggers are in place, execution might be risky

This stage can go on for any timeframe, from days to months to years, based on the characteristic of the company. The understanding of TREE Analogy will help you here.

The most interesting companies are a BOWLING ALLEY, which is undergoing subtle changes within it and are working on future earnings growth triggers. Just like in Bowling Alley, they put down pins like distribution network, branding, improving management, etc. which help businesses scale faster in the future.

So, should we pick the bottom in Stage 1?

Many smart investors who understand value, if they do their homework properly, will know that they might get the lowest price for business if things go in the right direction. So why not go all in?

There is a powerful concept of the opportunity cost of the capital and the time value of money. Even though we might pick a bottom or near-bottom price, we never know how long this consolidation will last or how long the execution of earnings growth triggers will take. This will not help us compound our money efficiently.

And often, this information is restricted only to the insiders, and it is very difficult to make an objective buying decision. Therefore, it is always prudent to revisit these companies when the execution starts.

As Mark Minervini mentions in his book *Trade Like a Stock Market Wizard*:

"My goal is not to buy at the lowest or cheapest price but at the "right" price, just as the stock is ready to move significantly higher. Trying to pick a bottom is unnecessary and a waste of time; it misses the whole point."

AVOID HOPE STORIES

This phase also gives birth to many hopeful investors. These are the ones who just get in by looking at the so-called cheap prices but get little growth. Even if growth may be far away or non-existent, these investors keep holding the shares for a long time, hoping someday something will happen. This, in my view, is just an illusion of value, particularly in a country like India. My observation is market values incremental growth and not value without growth.

This scenario also occurs when Banyan Trees transition into Mango Trees, i.e., the quality remains intact, but the growth rates slow down. This is often referred to as quality traps in the investing parlance. It's like just looking in the rear mirror and hoping that it will continue moving forward in the future.

STAGE 2 - ACCUMULATION PHASE: MEGA COMPOUNDING

At this stage, the market has been stable for a while and is moving higher. The early majority are getting on the bandwagon.

Here, the base breakout is crucial. What are breakouts? And why do they happen? A majority of investors wait for a fundamental trigger (capacity expansion, demerger, buyback), re-rating or tailwind for the next level of growth. When it's about to materialize, demand picks up in a short while. And this results in a breakout.

CHARACTERISTICS OF STAGE 2:

- Price breaks out of the accumulation phase in a range breakout after base formation
- Price forms higher highs and higher lows (Dow Theory)
- Short-term moving averages are above long-term moving averages, e.g., 20 DMA is above 50 DMA, and 50 DMA is above 200 DMA
- There are more up days than down days
- The average volume on up days is much higher than the average volume on down days

DMA = Daily Moving Averages

NEVER IGNORE STAGE 2 IN ALL-TIME HIGH TERRITORY

What happens when a stock enters from Stage 1 to Stage 2 with a price volume breakout and enters a new all-time high territory? It signifies the zone of least resistance. There is no pain. Each investor in that stock is sitting on a profit and thus, there is no incentive to sell. Supply remains limited as the existing shareholders want to ride their winners, and the price movements accelerate.

This is a powerful territory where we should closely study the fundamental triggers and take advantage of zones of least resistance. Most of the time, if a stock is hitting an all-time high, it's for a reason. Know the fundamental trigger, build the conviction and make the most of this phase.

As also stated earlier, we should pay close attention to buying volumes. There should be a significant increase in buying volume (at least 2x-3x of average volumes over the past few weeks) during this phase.

One should be cautious of breakouts that happen at a very low volume. Again, it's all about increasing the odds in your favor. Breakouts with little increase in volume can also succeed, but the probabilities (and hence, the risk-reward equations) are not in your favor.

Another important point is to respect Primary Trend. In bear markets, the probability of breakouts succeeding decreases drastically. It's simply stacking probability to have odds in our favor.

STAGE 3 - DISTRIBUTION PHASE: MAIN STREET

In the third phase of the market cycle, sellers dominate. This part of the cycle is identified by a period in which the bullish sentiment of the previous phase turns into a mixed sentiment. Prices can often stay locked in a trading range that can last a few weeks or even months. When this phase is over, the market reverses its direction. Classic patterns like double and triple tops, and head and shoulders patterns, are examples of movements that occur during the distribution phase.

EXAMPLES OF STAGE ANALYSIS:

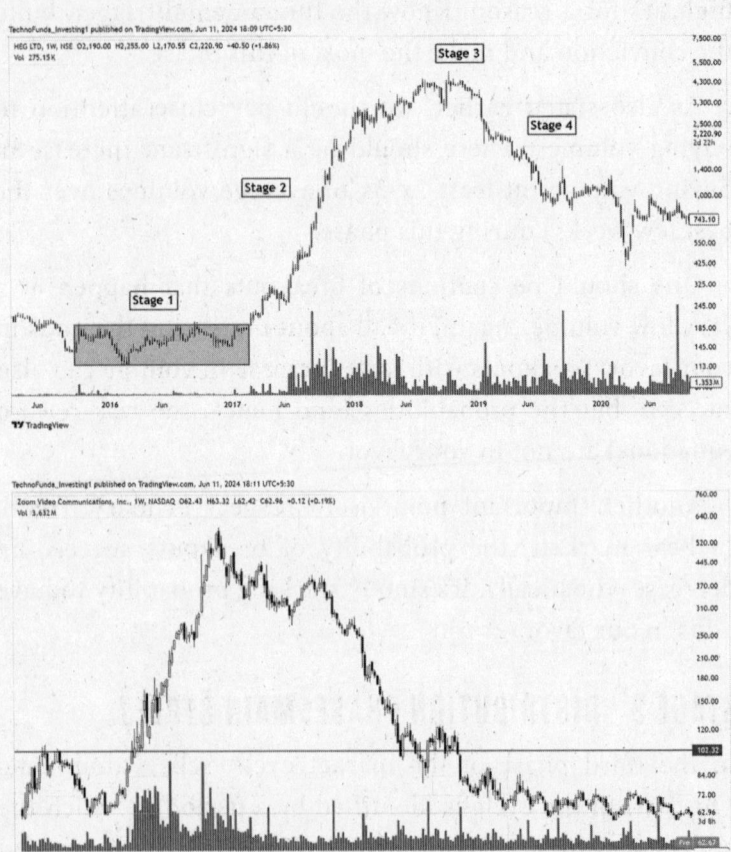

STAGE 4 - DECLINING PHASE: LAGGARDS

As we have learned earlier in this chapter, everything is cyclical - Nothing is permanent. So is the case with earnings growth and business momentum. There are several reasons why companies will stagnate and ultimately, even growth will taper.

Some sectors might get saturated due to high penetration or disruption forces or companies might face increased competition. Business models evolve, and so do the ways of doing business. Companies that do not evolve or are slow to evolve undergo a Declining Phase and are often termed as Laggards, i.e., Stage 4.

KEY CHARACTERISTICS OF STAGE 4:

- Price breaks down with severe down moves
- Price forms a series of lower highs and lower lows (Dow Theory)
- Short-term moving averages are below long-term moving averages, e.g., 20 DMA is below 50 DMA, and 50 DMA is below 200 DMA
- There are more down days than up days
- The average volume on down days is much higher than the average volume on up days

WHAT DOES THIS ALL MEAN?

The ideal way is to do fundamental research using a 4-cylinder model during stage 1, but not buy yet. This way, there is ample time to do research and you are well prepared to seize the opportunity when stage 2 begins, as your research is already done.

It makes sense for institutions to accumulate during consolidation before breakout (otherwise, they will not get the opportunity). But for retail investors, it's best to wait until the consolidation is completed. This is because consolidation can last for weeks or months, or even years.

As a retail investor, we can quickly enter within a fraction of seconds. Then why waste the opportunity cost of capital with no returns?

Later, stage 3 is where one should be extremely cautious and once you can spot it correctly, it's even a good time to book profits, either fully or partially. Finally, stage 4 is when we should not participate. This stage is much easier to identify than stage 3. One should not fall into a hope story in stage 4, nor should one average down. The only thing to remember during stage 4 - STAY OUT.

CHAPTER SUMMARY

- The more time an individual spends in the investing world, the more they appreciate the cyclicity of things.
- By keenly observing price movements, the volume traded, and the fundamentals of the company, one can generally classify these cycles into four stages:
    - Stage 1 - Basing Phase: Bowling Alley
    - Stage 2 - Accumulation Phase: Mega Compounding
    - Stage 3 - Distribution Phase: Main Street
    - Stage 4 - Declining Phase: Laggards

STAGE 1- BASE PHASE: BOWLING ALLEY

- It is a phase of equilibrium. Cases, where it happens, include when a business has low growth without any incremental growth triggers/ when it is working on future growth triggers. Still, the execution is uncertain and in cases when an overall market condition is lackluster. Stage 1 characteristics:
    - Overall buying and selling activity will be lackluster
    - Price movement is in equilibrium with relatively much lower volumes as bulls & bears are in equilibrium
    - The ratio of up days to down days is pretty much equal
    - There are no trends, and stocks keep consolidating

- The stock price is below key moving averages
- The average volume on up days is almost equal to the average volume on down days

UNDERLYING REASONS FOR SUCH

- Market participants are never in a hurry to buy and wait for earning growth triggers
- Because of the lack of any institutional buying interest
- Even with potential earnings triggers being in place, execution becomes risky

Should investors go for Stage 1? Yes, if one does his/her homework well, they might get the lowest price for the business.

STAGE 2 - ACCUMULATION PHASE: MEGA COMPOUNDING

- In this stage, the market has begun getting stable and moving higher

STAGE 2 CHARACTERISTICS

- Price breaks out of the accumulation phase in a range breakout after base formation
- Price forms a series of higher highs and higher lows (Dow Theory)
- Short-term moving averages are above long-term moving averages, e.g., 20 DMA is above 50 DMA, and 50 DMA is above 200 DMA
- There are more up days than down days
- The average volume on up days is much higher than the average volume on down days

STAGE 3 - DISTRIBUTION PHASE: MAIN STREET

- In this stage, sellers start dominating
- The stage is marked by the period in which the bullish sentiment of the previous phase turns into mixed sentiment
- Various patterns that occur in this phase include double and triple tops and head and should patterns

STAGE 4 - DECLINING PHASE: LAGGARDS

- Nothing is stagnant, and in business, companies are stagnant, and eventually, growth tapers

STAGE 4 KEY CHARACTERISTICS INCLUDE:

- Price breaks down with severe down moves
- Price forms a series of lower highs and lower lows (Dow Theory)
- Short-term moving averages are below long-term moving averages, e.g., 20 DMA is below 50 DMA, and 50 DMA is below 200 DMA
- There are more down days than up days
- The average volume on down days is much higher than the average volume on up days

In stage 1, investors should do fundamental research but don't buy yet. In stage 2, investors should consider the research given, and in 3, one should be extremely cautious. Once it's spotted correctly, it creates a great time to book profits. In the last stage, one should be keen not to fall into a business hope story of one day excelling.

YOUR REFLECTIONS

(Reflect on what you have learned and pen down your thoughts)

_____

_____

_____

_____

_____

_____

_____

_____

_____

_____

_____

_____

_____

_____

_____

_____

_____

_____

CHAPTER SIX

CORE AND SATELLITE

"To suppose that safety-first consists in having a small gamble in many different [companies] where I have no information to reach a good judgment, as compared with a substantial stake in a company where one's information is adequate, strikes me as a travesty of investment policy."
—**John Maynard Keynes**
Letter to F.C. Scott, February 6, 1942[1]

SETTING PORTFOLIO GOALS

As an investor, we should have goals of compounding and generating portfolio returns.

The simplest goal one can keep is beating benchmark returns by a minimum of 10%. In the Indian context, if we consider Nifty/Sensex, the average returns have been in the range of 15%. In essence, we are aiming for 25%

---

[1]Donald Moggridge, ed., *The Collected Writings of John Maynard Keynes* (New York: Cambridge University Press, 1983)

compounding, i.e. on an average, your money should double in at least every 3 years.

This might not look that great, but as Ramesh Damani has explained in his famous lecture - If you compound 10 lakh at this rate, it will become 100 crores in 30 years. This is the magic of compounding.

HOW TO ACHIEVE AT LEAST 2X RETURNS IN 3 YEARS?

After understanding the tree analogy of Quality vs. Growth, one should allocate capital to "Banyan" type businesses.

If you have a 100% portfolio allocated to such businesses, there are some challenges:

- Generally, these businesses, at large, would be available at reasonable valuations only during a bear market, so we have to time the market and sit on cash until the opportunity arises

- During the Bull Market, these businesses will be priced to perfection and they will have a substantial premium attached, so there is a chance of lower returns if we give a higher entry valuation

- There is a significant risk of de-rating if there are earnings de-growth (compared to market expectations), and hence, portfolio underperformance

- There is little room to outperform the index with a huge margin

Given the above scenario, there is a low probability of generating 25% compounding either by sitting on cash for a long duration or by entering at a very high valuation.

Of course, if you are lucky and reading this in the bear market, and just got started, you may achieve it. Below is an illustration of what can happen when you compound at 25% every year.

Power of Doubling money every three years
(without even fresh capital addition)[2]

AGE	₹
25	10 Lakh
28	20 Lakh
31	40 Lakh
34	80 Lakh
37	1.6 Crore
40	3.2 Crore
43	6.4 Crore
46	12.8 Crore
49	25.6 Crore
52	51.2 Crore
55	102.4 Crore

WHAT SHOULD BE DONE TO SOLVE THIS?

The solution is to construct CORE:SATELLITE Portfolio. I prefer keeping a 70:30 allocation.

---

[2]Vishal Mittal and Saurabh Basrar, *Masterclass with Super-Investors -Ramesh Damani Interview* (New Delhi: Maple Press India, 2018)

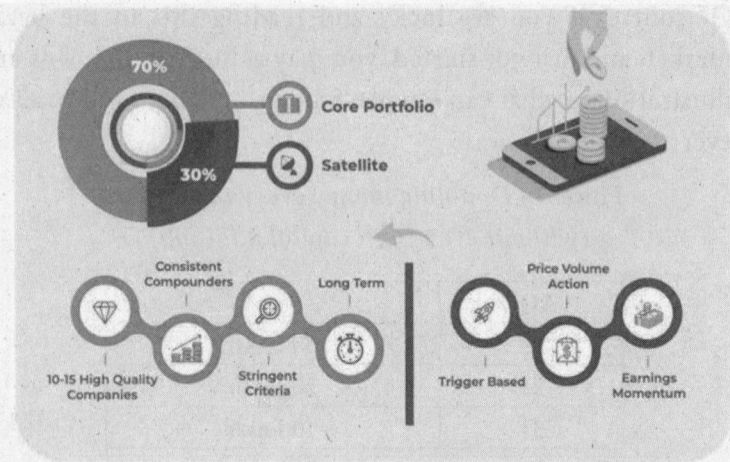

In this case, the CORE portfolio consists of 10-15 high-quality businesses, i.e., Banyan Trees.

While the Satellite portfolio consists of potential winners, which might be the following categories:

- Potential Mango to Banyan transition: Growth coming back in high RoCE businesses

- Potential Bamboo Trees: Increase in RoCE and Growth either temporary/permanent

- Palm Trees: Cyclical businesses transitioning from low to high RoCE/Growth and vice versa

- Any such similar situation where business is potentially improving and in transition

Satellite portfolio companies have the potential to give great payoffs if they play out as expected. But there is a little edge in terms of understanding the business due to the inherent nature of business.

The purpose of the Satellite portfolio is to constantly look for future core portfolio stocks and simultaneously keep learning about new businesses, as the churn in the core portfolio is minimal.

Satellite Portfolio consists of potential winners, which might be following categories

Potential Mango to Banyan transition: Growth coming back in high ROCE businesses	**Potential Bamboo Trees:** Increase in ROCE and Growth either temporary/permanent
Palm Trees: Cyclical businesses transitioning from low to high ROCE/Growth and vice versa	Any such similar situation where business is potentially improving and in transition

"So I think it was just looking at different companies and I always thought if you looked at ten companies, you'd find one that's interesting, if you'd look at 20, you'd find two, or if you look at hundred, you'll find ten. The person that turns over the most rocks wins the game."

—Peter Lynch[3]

Another key point here is that the satellite portfolio goes to cash during down-trending markets. Hence, it creates an automatic hedge that gives mental peace and the opportunity

[3]https://www.pbs.org/wgbh/pages/frontline/shows/betting/pros/lynch.html

to take advantage of steep market falls to accumulate core portfolio companies.

STRENGTH IS EVERYTHING

A powerful concept of Relative Strength calculates performance vs. underlying index under comparison for a given timeframe. If stock returns are the same as the underlying index, the stock will have zero relative strength.

As soon as stock returns outperform the returns of the underlying index for a given timeframe, relative strength becomes greater than zero.

While selecting stocks for investing, generally, it is prudent to screen stocks showing strong relative strength. It's not a good idea to buy stocks if the relative strength is in negative territory (i.e. less than zero).

Relative strength further helps us to increase the odds in our favor. It indicates which side of the demand-supply equation is tilting.

There are mainly 3 scenarios around relative strength for a given timeframe under consideration:

(1) The index is moving upwards with positive returns and stock is outperforming with even higher returns

(2) The index is flat, but still stock is outperforming the index with positive returns

(3) The index is falling with negative returns, but the stock is positive, flat or has fallen lesser than the index

Below is an example of BSE that explains base breakout on a daily chart coupled with increasing volume towards breakout and relative strength line crossing above zero. The stock has become more than 4x in less than 1 year.

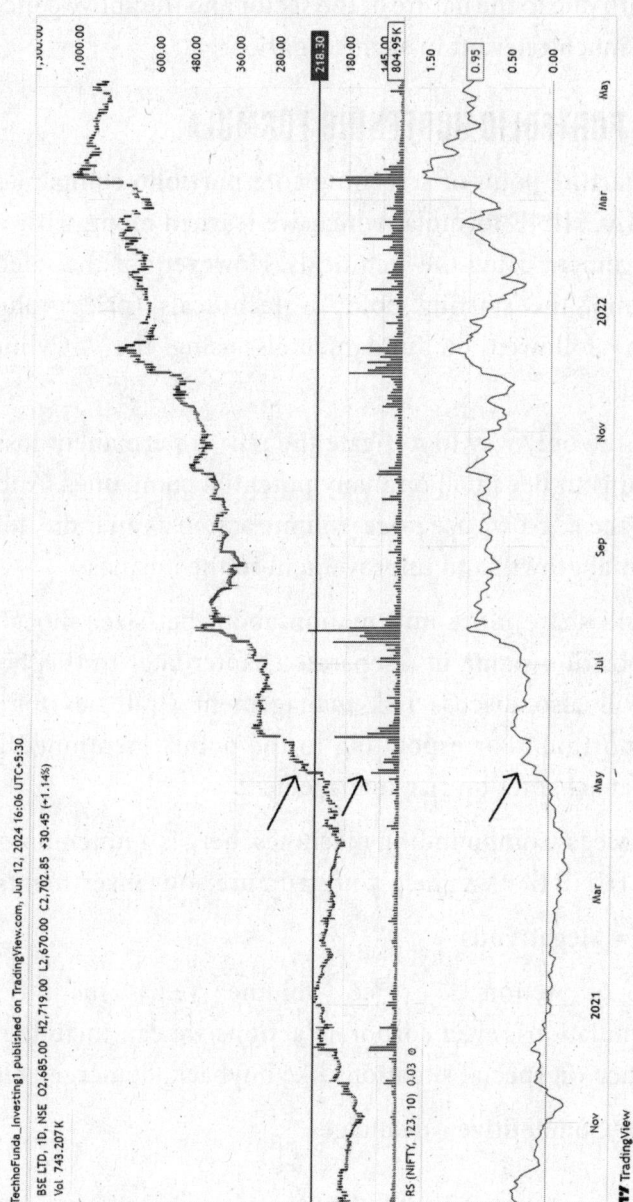

During the market correction or bear market, defensive stocks like utilities, FMCG, etc., will naturally show relative strength due to the nature of the sector and the above concept is not much relevant in such scenarios.

CORE PORTFOLIO SCREENING FORMULA

The starting point of screening core portfolio companies is the MACHINE formula, which we learned along with risk management using the technicals. However, for the satellite portfolio, the starting point is technicals (price volume action) followed by fundamentals using the 4-Cylinder Model.

So, the only way to mitigate the risk of permanent loss of capital is to bet small on many potential companies. And to bring the edge, we use price-volume action as an indicator of potential growth and improvement in the business.

I will share more information about bet size, allocation and position sizing in a separate chapter later in this book. We will also discuss risk management strategies for the core portfolio corresponding to the points mentioned in a separate chapter on risk management.

In Mega Compounding machines, here is a mnemonic for MACHINE that can help you structure your investments:

M = Megatrends

A = Action - price volume (e.g., institutional accumulation), even corporate actions we can include here to touch on special situations like buyback, demerger, etc.

C = Competitive Advantages

H = High Quality (usually measured by High Return on Capital Employed)

I = Improvement

N = New Developments (new products/management/new price highs)

E = Execution of Earnings Growth Triggers

The mnemonic for MACHINE that will help you structure your investments in Mega Compounding Machines

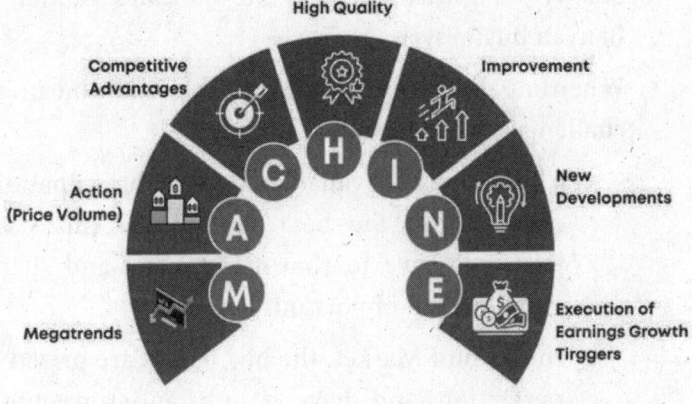

CHAPTER SUMMARY

SETTING PORTFOLIO GOALS

- Investors should have goals in terms of compounding and generating portfolio returns.

- One simple goal that investors should keep includes beating benchmarked returns by a minimum of 10%.

- One can attain at least 2x returns in three years. Such can happen through utilizing the tree analogy of quality vs. growth, where one allocates capital in Banyan businesses.

- When one allocates a 100% portfolio in such a business, challenges faced include:

  - The business is available at reasonable valuations only during the bear market. In this case, investors have to time the market and sit on cash until an opportunity arises

  - In the Bull Market, the businesses are prized to perfection and have a substantial premium attached. Given a higher entry valuation, a chance of lower returns exists

  - Face a risk of de-rating when earning de-growth occurs, and hence portfolio underperforms

  - A little room to outperform the index with a huge margin

- There are two types of portfolios, including core and satellite portfolios. Core maintains a 70% while Satellite maintains a 0-30%. The core includes 10-15 high-quality companies. It has consistent compounders, stringent selection criteria, and a long-time horizon. On the other hand, Satellite is trigger-based, involves price volume action, and has earnings momentum.

- The satellite portfolio examines a future business while the core portfolio stock keeps learning about new business.

- Satellite potential winners:

  - Potential Mango to Banyan transition (Growth comes in high ROCE business)

  - Potential bamboo trees (Increase in ROCE and growth, either temporal or permanent

  - Palm trees-cyclical business

CORE PORTFOLIO SCREENING FORMULA

- The MACHINE formula starts with core portfolio screening.

- MACHINE, in this case, means:

  - M = Megatrends

  - A = Action - price volume (e.g., institutional accumulation), even corporate actions we can include here to touch on special situations like buyback, demerger, etc.

  - C = Competitive Advantages

  - H = High Quality (usually measured by High Return on Capital Employed)

  - I = Improvement

- N = New Developments (new products/management/new price highs)
- E = Execution Of Earnings Growth Triggers
- The only way to mitigate investment risks is to bet small on many potential companies.
- In the core portfolio, business growth is examined through potential growth and business improvement.

YOUR REFLECTIONS

(Reflect on what you have learned and pen down your
thoughts)

_____

_____

_____

_____

_____

_____

_____

_____

_____

_____

_____

_____

_____

_____

_____

_____

_____

_____

_____

CHAPTER SEVEN
MEGATRENDS

"There's a model that I call "surfing"—when a surfer
gets up and catches the wave and just stays there,
he can go a long, long time."
—Charlie Munger

Understanding the big picture is very important before going deeper into analyzing individual businesses. It's all about increasing your odds and ensuring you are not facing headwinds. This big picture is the driving force of a giant shift that can keep happening for years or even decades. This whooping shift is called megatrends.

These are long-term structural trends with irreversible consequences. India's IT services revolution, the shift from PSU banks to private sector banks, unorganized to organized economy, discretionary consumption theme, Indian pharmaceutical APIs, specialty chemicals manufacturing shift from China to India, etc., are all examples of megatrends.

Other synonyms for megatrends are value migration and sector tailwinds. These should not be confused with short/medium term, temporary, cyclical trends, or those that occur regularly in sectors like steel, sugar, commodity/bulk chemicals, paper, etc.

Now let us understand why we need tailwinds at all? If the company is great, it will do well despite the sector tailwinds, right? Consider flying a kite on Makar Sankranti (an Indian festival dedicated to Lord Sun)- even if the kite is thin, lightweight and aerodynamic in structure, it will not fly if there is no wind!

Consider swimming: if the tidal currents are in the direction opposing you, you must swim much harder. If there are no waves, it is neutral and your swimming pace is the only determinant of your speed. If the wave is with you, you can swim at a high speed even with little of your own force. As the saying goes, the rising tide lifts all boats.

To Expand Wealth you need to Align with Powerful Forces

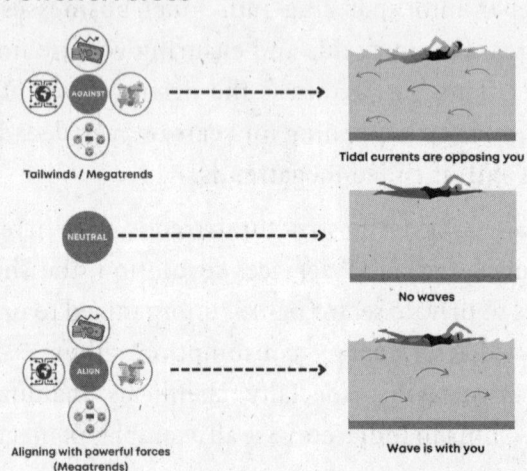

Tailwinds / Megatrends

Tidal currents are opposing you

NEUTRAL

No waves

Aligning with powerful forces (Megatrends)

Wave is with you

Therefore, to create wealth through mega compounding, one needs to align with powerful forces. It keeps expanding the size of opportunities for businesses and creates strong acceleration.

> *"One should identify a fish in the ocean and*
> *not a crocodile in a pond."*
> —*Vijay Kedia*[1]

There are 3 Powerful forces that create strong acceleration:

1. A positive trend in the primary economic cycle

2. Tailwinds in sector

3. Strong underlying drivers contributing to the megatrend

3 Powerful Forces which create strong Acceleration

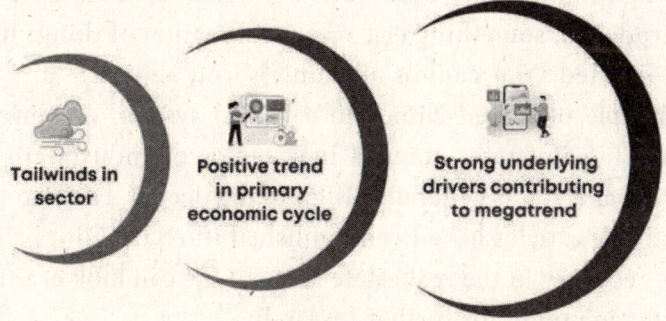

Tailwinds in sector

Positive trend in primary economic cycle

Strong underlying drivers contributing to megatrend

For example, India's economy is undergoing strong economic growth and sectors like Financials have strong

---

[1]Vishal Mittal and Saurabh Basrar, *Masterclass with Super-Investors - Vijay Kedia Interview* (New Delhi: Maple Press India, 2018)

tailwinds coupled with underlying drivers like digitalization, mobile penetration, internet connectivity, urbanization, formalization of the economy, etc. This megatrend has created huge wealth which can be observed in many companies in this sector.

> *"One of the lessons your management has learned— and, unfortunately, sometimes re-learned—is the importance of being in businesses where tailwinds prevail rather than headwinds."*
>
> *—Warren Buffett*

So how can one identify megatrends? John Naisbitt, the pioneer of this concept, writes, "Why are we so confident that content analysis is an effective way to monitor social change? Simply stated, because the news hole in a newspaper is a closed system. For economic reasons, the amount of space devoted to news in a newspaper does not change significantly over time. So, when something new is introduced, something else or a combination of things must be omitted. You cannot add unless you subtract. It is the principle of forced-choice in a closed system." When you find frequent talks about a new sector or industry in the newspapers, it is generally a sign to dig deeper. For example, multiple articles have been published in recent times about the recovery in the real estate sector. One can look at this as a starting point for further research.

Another way is through the price volume action of multiple companies in a sector. We will study this further in the next chapter.

One megatrend going on for the future is the shift from atoms to bits. Something like Airbnb, they have no real estate and they are the largest accommodation provider. In the same way, if you think about Uber, they don't own any cars; if you think about Alibaba, they do not own any inventory. So, these are the emerging platform businesses coming up.

UBER'S FLYWHEEL

As per the 26th Motilal Oswal Wealth Creation Study- "India is on the cusp of a digital revolution. For a population of 1.3 billion, India's wireless subscriber base is at 1.2 billion and broadband subscriber base at 0.8 billion. Almost 0.75 billion users access the internet through their mobile phones. Even as the customer base is rising, the corporate and investment climate is also getting conducive by the day. Entrepreneurs are conjuring up digital business ideas across domains – from fintech to foodtech to edutech. They are backed by a whole host of venture capital and private equity funds, leading to the emergence of several unicorns (companies with a valuation of USD 1 bn or higher), numbering over 70 at the last count. The Indian government too is doing its bit. Almost 99% of India's adult population now has Aadhaar (unique identification number). In 2016, the government launched a Unified Payment Interface (UPI), enabling peer-to-peer interbank transfers at zero cost. Under a scheme called Jan Dhan, over the past 7 years, 430 million low-income strata people now have bank accounts, a trigger for widespread financial and commercial inclusion. On the stock market front, regulator SEBI (Securities & Exchange Board of India) has relaxed its regulations to permit the listing of loss-making companies as well. Thus, India is all set for an exciting Bits era."

In sync with our hypothesis of price reflecting the actions of smart buyers and the collective wisdom of the market, consider this: Of the top 10 market cap companies in 1995 in the USA, Microsoft is the only company to remain in the current list as well.[2]

Exhibit 2 **Top 10 US companies by Market Cap – Current and 1995 (USD bn)**

Company	Current	Company	1995	Current
Apple	2,712	General Electric	120	104
Microsoft	2,482	AT&T	103	163
Alphabet	1,888	Exxon Mobil	100	253
Amazon.com	1,779	Coca-Cola	94	227
Tesla	1,150	Merck & Co	81	189
Meta Platforms	903	Altria Group	75	78
Nvidia Corp	817	Procter & Gamble	57	350
Berkshire Hathaway	619	Johnson & Johnson	55	411
J P Morgan Chase	469	Microsoft	52	2,482
Visa	422	Walmart	51	392

---

[2]Motilal Oswal, Atoms to Bits, 26th Annual Wealth Creation Study (2016-2021)

CASE STUDY OF CDSL:

CDSL is listed depository where our shares and other important documents are being held in dematerialized format. This is an example of platform business with huge operating leverage. It has been beneficiary of confluence of megatrends i.e., financialization of savings and digitalization.[3]

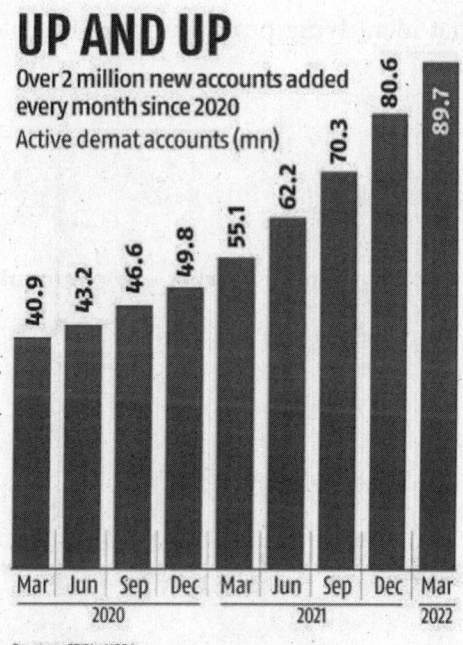

UP AND UP

Over 2 million new accounts added every month since 2020

Active demat accounts (mn)

Mar	Jun	Sep	Dec	Mar	Jun	Sep	Dec	Mar
40.9	43.2	46.6	49.8	55.1	62.2	70.3	80.6	89.7
2020				2021				2022

Source: CDSL, NSDL

During the last few years, there has been a huge surge in the number of Demat accounts on both CDSL and its unlisted

---

[3]https://www.business-standard.com/article/markets/india-s-demat-account-tally-up-63-to-89-7-million-in-fy22-shows-data-122041401088_1.html

competitor, NSDL. Shareholders have been rewarded handsomely due to excellent profit growth. The share price of CDSL surged almost 9x from the lows of March 2020 to its high in December 2021, in less than 2 years. Quarterly, EPS jumped from ₹ 2 to ₹ 6 during the same period. And remember, these are sticky businesses with recurring revenue streams. So, the incremental impact on valuation will be huge.

This is what identifying powerful megatrends can do for you!

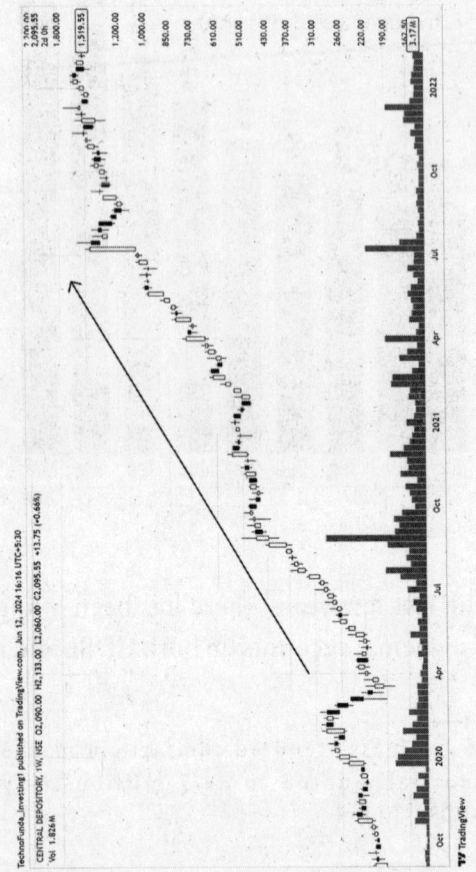

These businesses also have so many optionalities due to the digitalization megatrend.

I was fortunate to identify this business early on in Dec-2019 and had listed these optionalities:[4]

 vivek_mashrani

CDSL I believe is at a very interesting sweet spot with multiple income streams + lot of optionality embedded with huge opportunity size.

While some of the known regular segments provide annuity based revenue, some cyclical (eg. listing etc.), and then there is transaction based revenue stream based on shares which are transacted.

The second part on optionality is quite interesting with below legs which has huge opportunity size:

1. CCRL: CDSL commodity repository Ltd (subsidiary with JV with BSE and MCX) which caters to commodity segment and I believe this is at very nascent stage in India

https://www.bseindia.com/markets/MarketInfo/DispNewNoticesCirculars.aspx?page=20190213-43 25

2. CDSL Insurance Repository: This has huge scope and high probability that this will become mandatory in coming years. Given the population and penetration of insurance in our country, even with very tiny fees, this can be good incremental revenue stream in future

3. NAD: National Academic Depository which caters to academic records; This has started quite well and has huge scope; This will lead to faster admission processes, lesser record keeping and thus should be good incentive for colleges to outsource

We have seen how digitalizing of unlisted shares has now become quite significant revenue stream for the company.

As far as there is no new entrant and CDSL keeps playing smartly by gaining market share from NSDL, these optionality looks quite good. Counter-views welcome.

Disclosure: Hold tracking position

Disclaimer: This is not a recommendation to buy or sell. Kindly consider this as an educational case study. Our family members are currently invested in CDSL while I am writing this book.

[4]https://forum.valuepickr.com/t/cdsl-stock-for-our-children/18078/88?u=vivek_mashrani

CHAPTER SUMMARY

- The key to analyzing businesses is focusing on the impetus of the enterprises, also known as the megatrend.

- The revolution in India's IT services, the shift from PSU to private sector banks, and the shift from specialty chemicals manufacturing from China to India are all megatrends.

- Other terms for megatrends are value migration and sector tailwinds.

- If you want to create wealth through mega compounding, you must be in sync with powerful forces to expand opportunities in your business and develop strong acceleration.

- The three powerful forces to identify are a positive trend in the primary economic cycle, tailwinds in the sector, and strong underlying drivers contributing to the megatrend.

- One example of a megatrend in India is in the financial sector.

- The Indian financial sector is currently exhibiting positive economic growth.

- Finance sector enterprises also make huge profits from notable tailwinds and underlying drivers like digitalization, mobile penetration, internet connectivity, urbanization, and economy formalization.

- There are also notable sources of identifying megatrends.

- One source of identifying megatrends is by analyzing newspaper content where there is always information about the industry and new sectors.

- However, according to John Naisbitt, a pioneer of the megatrend concept, content analysis alone is not feasible in identifying megatrends because it also highlights other social issues, limiting depth coverage of the former.

- Naisbitt asserts that it is because of the closed newspaper system, which limits newspaper space, that the volume of the information displayed remains fixed, leaving out content.

- Newspapers must delete some of their information to accommodate new data.

- You can use the newspaper to identify megatrends and then carry out in-depth research using other content-heavy sources because of the depth scarcity.

- Price volume action is another way of identifying megatrends.

- There is also an emerging megatrend in business platforms like Uber, Airbnb, or Alibaba, which requires no inventory or property ownership.

YOUR REFLECTIONS

(Reflect on what you have learned and pen down your thoughts)

_____

_____

_____

_____

_____

_____

_____

_____

_____

_____

_____

_____

_____

_____

_____

_____

_____

_____

_____

CHAPTER EIGHT
ACTION

"The big money is not in the buying and the selling, but in waiting."
—Charlie Munger

Any economic activity generally is based on the law of supply and demand. And markets are no different. Every single second, each transaction on the stock exchange ultimately reflects demand-supply factors. Price is the result of demand and supply that we see even in stock markets, just like any other commodity we purchase.

Investing returns are simply the difference between the price at which you buy and the price at which you sell (net of transaction costs and any dividends, etc.). Hence, understand actions that can ultimately increase the price in the future.

Some examples of these actions that can signify an improvement in demand are:

- Promoter Buying
- Institutional Buying

- The Action of Management to execute effectively
- Prudence of Management in taking leverage

Investors also need to pay attention to a concept called FREE FLOAT. One needs to understand that the supply of shares is freely available in the market for transactions out of the total number of shares outstanding.

The lesser the percentage and number of shares available freely, the higher will be the fluctuation in terms of share price movement (on both sides). Many investors miss this simple demand-supply logic while investing. Generally, in my anecdotal experience, the best-performing stocks have floats under 1 crore shares.

The "float"—the number of company shares available to trade in the open market—is a key determinant of how easy it will be for momentum traders to manipulate the stock to higher levels. These are the shares in the public domain not held by company insiders.

One should look at the volume-to-float ratio, i.e. average daily traded volume divided by free float. If the float is 15 lakh shares while the average daily volume is 75000 shares (V/F of 0.05), it is unlikely that the stock will move wildly until there is a spike in volume. But if the float is 10 lakh shares and the average daily volume is 2 lakh shares (V/F of 0.2), the available float will be 'eaten up' quickly. So, more likely, there will be dramatic price swings.

Less liquidity can give faster up-move, but it comes with the additional risk of a faster downside. Risk management is key in such situations.

PROMOTER BUYING ACTIVITY

"Insiders might sell their shares for any number of reasons, but they buy them for only one: they think the price will rise."
—**Peter Lynch**[1]

Insiders know the company in and out and have much more knowledge than the outsider market participants. If they are buying their own shares, it is a sign they are confident of better performance and a higher share price in the future. Further, not only insider buying is an indicator of future fundamental success at the company level, but it also promotes significant levels of investor confidence in the stock. This confidence ultimately translates into higher multiples on earnings, resulting in much higher stock prices. Peter Lynch writes in his book *One Up on Wall Street*, "There's no better tip-off to the probable success of a stock than that people in the company are putting their own money into it."

Most times, when the promoter of the company buys shares from the open market or the company is doing buybacks at attractive signs, it's a good sign. Of course, we must look at other MACHINE criteria, not just look at this criterion in isolation. Other than the promoter, even purchases from the CFO are a good sign. As Gautam Baid writes, "Pay special attention when you see a chief financial officer buying stock from the open market. It's generally not in their DNA to think like an owner."[2]

---

[1]https://www.investopedia.com/articles/02/061202.asp#:~:text=One%20of%20the%20greatest%20investors,six%2Dmonth%20period%3B%20therefore%2C)
[2]Gautam Baid, *The Joys of Compounding* (New York, Columbia University Press, 2020)

One also needs to look at the percentage of buying vs. overall percentage holding. If it's too tiny, in a broader context, it has little meaning and sometimes can be due to manipulative intent as well. One should see that the size of the purchases is large in relation to the insider's remuneration. For example, even a small insider purchase of ₹ 5 lakh can be meaningful if the buyer's salary is ₹ 30 lakh. As Peter Lynch states, "Although it's a nice gesture for the CEO or the corporate president with the million-dollar salary to buy a few thousand shares of the company stock, it's more significant when employees at the lower echelons add to their positions. If you see someone with a $45,000 annual salary buying $10,000 worth of stock, you can be sure it's a meaningful vote of confidence. That's why I'd rather find seven vice presidents buying 1,000 shares apiece than the president buying 5,000."[3] In such cases, one should take notice and begin further research, especially if multiple executives are buying. This is called cluster buying; when multiple insiders from a management team make open-market purchases within a narrow period.

Lynch adds, "If the stock price drops after the insiders have bought, so that you have a chance to buy it cheaper than they did, so much the better for you."[4]

For example, as we can see from screener.in, promoters of Kabra Extrusion Technik were constantly and aggressively buying shares and increasing their shareholding.

---

[3]Peter Lynch, *One Up On Wall Street*, (New York: Simon & Schuster, 1989)
[4]Peter Lynch, *One Up On Wall Street*, (New York: Simon & Schuster, 1989)

Shareholding Pattern
Numbers in percentages

	Mar 2019	Jun 2019	Sep 2019	Dec 2019	Mar 2020	Jun 2020	Sep 2020	Dec 2020	Mar 2021	Jun 2021	Sep 2021	Dec 2021
Promoters +	57.32	57.32	57.58	57.58	57.68	57.86	57.84	58.03	58.56	59.03	59.46	60.22
FIIs +	0.47	0.47	0.41	0.81	0.97	0.97	0.97	0.97	0.80	0.72	1.01	0.95
DIIs +	0.03	0.03	0.02	0.04	0.01	0.01	0.01	0.01	0.01	0.01	0.01	0.01
Public +	42.19	42.19	41.99	41.56	41.34	41.34	41.18	40.99	40.63	40.24	39.52	38.82

Person	Quantity	Avg Price	Value in Rs. Lacs
Sep 2021			
Kolsite Industries Promoter Group	154,460	244	377
Jun 2021			
Kolsite Industries Promoter Group	69,707	184	128
May 2021			
Kolsite Industries Promoter Group	60,000	194	116
Shreevallabh G Kabra Promoter & Director	11,000	195	21
Mar 2021			
Kolsite Industries Promoter Group	58,701	152	89
Feb 2021			
Kolsite Industries Promoter Group	49,725	112	55

INSTITUTIONAL BUYING

Big demand gets created when big pockets start buying. These big pockets in markets are institutions. What are these institutions? They are domestic mutual funds, FIIs, big PMS houses, hedge funds, pension funds, sovereign wealth funds, AIFs, small cases, etc. The transaction volumes they bring are very large. The institutional buyers are, by far, the largest source of demand for stocks. Outperformers usually have institutional backing.

There are two demand triggers created by institutional buying:

1. When one or more institutions buy shares for the first time in the history of the company.

This one is special as this creates huge interest in the investor community, particularly if there are credible institutions buying. William O'Neil calls this analyzing the quality of institutional sponsorship.

Chatur: But why and when does it happen?

Aryan: Bingo Chatur, I am carried away by your inquisitiveness.

Generally, liquidity is a big hurdle for large institutions. If there are companies with an overall market cap of less than 2000-3000 crores and free float, which is even less than 500-1000 crores, it's difficult for institutions to enter. This is subjective, and there are exceptions. Second, they want to see consistency in performance and the company should pass a stringent due diligence process. Also, multiple retail investors and HNIs have a strategy of 'coat-tailing' and 'cloning' the portfolios of savvy fund managers. Their buying can create additional demand.

Especially note new positions. As O'Neil writes, "A significant new position taken by an institutional investor in the most recently reported period is generally more relevant than existing positions that have been held for some time. When a fund establishes a new position, the chances are that it will continue to add to that position and be less likely to sell it in the near future."[5]

Retail investors can get hugely rewarded if they can use this SWEET SPOT by buying shares of quality companies that can potentially cross this liquidity threshold and institutions get interested. Again, both fundamental analysis and technical analysis can spot such opportunities. One must also note that investment decisions should not be solely on potential institution buying but also all other MACHINE criteria of long-term growth should be followed.

2. When a company with existing institutions sees an increase in institutional holding and/or more institutions start buying.

These are generally mid to large companies with existing institutional ownership and the holding steadily goes up. Most times (not always), this shows higher conviction in the underlying company. Often even new institutional investors enter and buy shares.

This should be viewed alongside business performance, growth potential and management quality. Sometimes, just

---

[5]William O'Neil, *How to make money in stocks* (New York: McGraw Hill, 2009)

due to large-cap mandates, many institutions might buy matured companies. If we enter late in the party, when most institutions have entered, it might probably be too late and can give suboptimal returns.

Expectations of some institutions like foreign pension funds, etc., might be just capital protection with single-digit returns. As a retail investor, we might want to compound much better and have a better stock selection (companies with high growth potential).

One can get quarterly shareholding patterns from stock exchanges - BSE/NSE in India and check details under public shareholding.

THE ACTION OF MANAGEMENT TO EXECUTE EFFECTIVELY

Owner-Operators have their skin in the game, and an efficient capital allocation as an owner can create miracles for the company.

The typical public company vs. the owner-operator

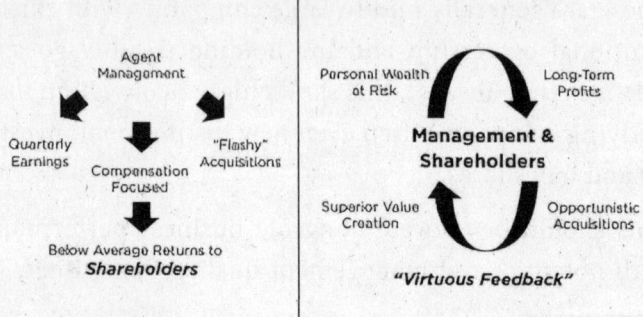

Source: Horizon Kinetics

Also, it is easier to hold onto a stock through the rough patches knowing we have a talented owner-operator with money on the line.

Ultimately, execution is the key. If there is a public company with "Puppet Managements" that are not agile, less growth-oriented and with interest at stake, there is a low probability of generating extraordinary returns.

Ultimately, the barometers of all these activities are - price and volume, popularly known as Price Volume Action.

PRICE VOLUME ACTION

Let's say we are finding the companies based on price volume action initially, which are going from stage one to stage two or sometimes even from stage three back to the continuation phase or stage two. Most times, when these companies are going from stage one to stage two, it is due to some fundamental trigger. Now, the problem is that the fundamental news is not yet known to the public, right? This is where we have the smart money getting in. And we also have people who are insiders, who have good experience around cycles and who are doing a lot of scuttlebutts, entering this very, very early. We, as retail investors, do not have such bandwidth or expertise. So this is where the price-volume action helps us. Basically, there is a price spurt in the stock, there is a surge in trading volumes, the stock comes near a 52-week high and then the news comes out in the public domain.

So, when the price breaks out of a consolidation band (base) with good volumes, this is where a TechnoFunda investor will first initiate a position. Stage one is more of a consolidation phase. This is the phase where the stock is not doing anything. And later, when it gets to stage two, this is known as an uptrend. Hence, it's very important to first identify that we are at the beginning of the trend. This is where the price-volume action helps us catch the transition from phase 1 to phase 2.

The second part comes into play when it's into stage two and the advancing phase. This advancing phase is when, most of the time, the news comes out. In this phase, a lot of research reports will start getting published. They will do earnings upgrades and all sorts of those things. A lot of euphoria will be there, and people will start talking about it on social media. This is where you know that your stage two has started. Many good value investors might think that they are right in picking up the company at the initial phase of stage one. But they are not able to ride stage two because they feel there's a lot of noise, and most of the time, even before the earnings come out, they have valuations that seemingly look very high. They feel, 'it is a 52-week high and valuation is very high'. Therefore, most people sell up on very small returns, right? 10-20-30% returns. But if you can write this properly, you can make multiple returns. It could be anywhere up to 40, 50 or 80X. You never know, right? Again, it depends totally upon how long the stage prevails. But if you can write it, and if it is really a big trend, you will make a killing out of it. And if this is coupled with good allocation, it will be a deadly combination.

Below is the case study of HLE Glascoat (earlier Swiss Glascoat). You can see the below chart and do this exercise to go through various news that came after the advancing phase. This became ~30x in less than 2 years. You too can compound like this if you follow the system I have shared.

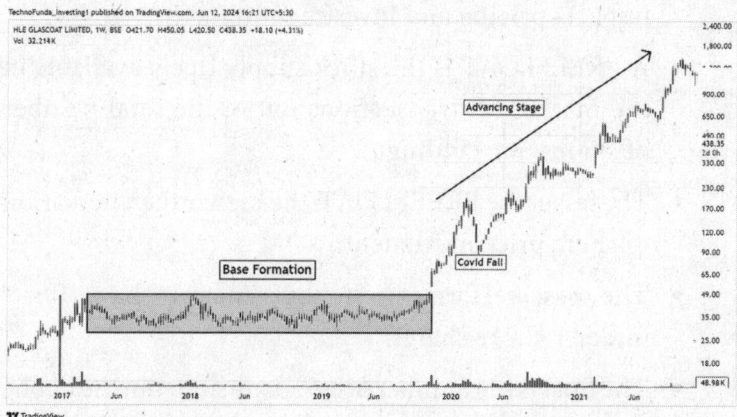

CHAPTER SUMMARY

- Markets and economic activities like stock exchange and transactions operate on supply and demand; this impacts pricing and investment returns.

- A FREEFLOAT is the stock supply freely available in the market for transactions out of the total number of shares outstanding.

- The lesser the FREEFLOAT, the higher the fluctuation in share price movement.

- The best-performing stocks generally have floats under 1 Crore shares.

- The float is the number of company shares in the public domain not held by company insiders available to trade in the open market; it determines how easily traders can manipulate the stock to higher levels.

- The daily volume of traded shares to float ratio determines the volatility of share pricing.

- Lesser liquidity means quick profits and higher losses risk.

- Promoter buying is when insiders buy their company's shares; it affects stock demand.

- Promoter buying indicates the future fundamental success of the shares, enhances investor confidence in the stock, and increases stock price.

- Look at the percentage of buying vs. the overall percentage of holding to determine the value of promoter buying.

- Demand also increases when big institutions like domestic mutual funds, FIIs, big PMS houses, hedge funds, pension funds, sovereign wealth funds, AIFs, small cases, and so forth buy stock.

- Institutional buying creates two demand triggers; when a credible institution makes its first stock purchase, it spikes interest in the investment community. More institutions start buying when a company with existing institutions adds its institutional holding.

- Stock demand also increases when owner-operators with sufficient capital are at the helm of the stock and can hold the stock value through rough patches; this concept is the action of management to execute effectively.

- The barometer of stock demand is the price volume action.

- Demand for shares increases when the stock price remains high without any news or fundamental drive over a long period.

YOUR REFLECTIONS

(Reflect on what you have learned and pen down your thoughts)

_____

_____

_____

_____

_____

_____

_____

_____

_____

_____

_____

_____

_____

_____

_____

_____

CHAPTER NINE
COMPETITIVE ADVANTAGE

"The guiding principle of value creation is that companies create value by using capital they raise from investors to generate future cash flows at rates of return exceeding the cost of capital (the rate investors require as payment). The faster companies can increase their revenues and deploy more capital at attractive rates of return, the more value they create. The combination of growth and return on invested capital (ROIC) relative to its cost is what drives value. Companies can sustain strong growth and high returns on invested capital only if they have a well-defined competitive advantage. This is how competitive advantage, the core concept of business strategy, links to the guiding principle of value creation [emphasis added]. The corollary of this guiding principle, known as the conservation of value, says anything that doesn't increase cash flows doesn't create value."

—Timothy Koller

If you are competing against many peers, you always need an edge to succeed. In kite flying, someone who has a sharp maanja (string) has a competitive advantage. Even someone flying the kite from the terrace of a taller building has an advantage. Most probably, these are the people who will cut the most kites.

Companies are no different. Outstanding companies with competitive advantages are popularized by Warren Buffett as having "Moats".

"A truly great business must have an enduring "moat" that protects excellent returns on invested capital."

—Warren Buffett

In business, a competitive advantage is an attribute that allows an organization to outperform its competitors.

Aryan: OMG, I did not realize that it is almost midnight. So, I better get going as you two must be bone-tired after the day's work. We can continue this on some other day.

Chatur: Not at all mentor Aryan, rather we are feeling awakened now. Please, we insist that you continue showering the wellspring of your wisdom on us. So far, we were living in ignorance and made many mistakes. But now, we certainly have our thinking caps on.

Ranjita: I am sorry, I too went with the flow and did not realize that it has been a couple of hours since we had our dinner. Let me brew some black tea for the three of us.

Aryan: Oh, that will be great Ranjita. Chatur, there is nothing wrong in making mistakes, as they say, to err is human. Even I made a boatload of mistakes, which I will be sharing later. But we should not make the same mistakes again. Mistakes or failures are the stepping stones to success. So, the faster we fail, the quicker we navigate to the superhighway of success.

By the way, you just now said the word cap, which has reminded me of another CAP in the world of investing.

The competitive advantage period (CAP) is the time during which a company generates returns on investment that significantly exceeds its cost of capital. Economic laws suggest that if a company earns supernormal returns on its invested capital, it will attract competitors who will accept lower returns, eventually driving down the overall industry returns to the economic cost of capital, and sometimes even below it. However, a company with great business and management sustains its superior rates of return and keeps extending its CAP. This creates incremental excess return both for the company and for its equity investors. The ability to maintain longer-than-average CAP comes from a moat.

Some very common forms of Moats are:

- **Strong Brand**: Branding is one of the powerful aspects that helps businesses keep competition at bay and helps to enhance pricing power. It takes time, effort and vision to build powerful brands.

Consider the case of Page Industries. They are primarily into the mid-premium innerwear segment and have created an aspirational brand in India. They have used a unique approach to branding and advertising.

In his book *The Unusual Billionaires*, Saurabh Mukherjea has dissected this strategy:

Firstly, its advertising campaigns have consistently been high-impact affairs, like 'Just Jockeying' in FY2010-14 and 'Jockey or Nothing' launched in FY2015. Secondly, Page has placed significant emphasis on in-store advertising, to the extent that Jockey advertisements cover the bulk in-store advertising space at most multi-brand outlets (MBOs). Thirdly, in a neat play on the worldview of Indians, Page has consistently used Caucasian models in its advertising and thus firmly entrenched its brand recall as an international brand.[1]

Coupled with excellent capital allocation, high return ratios and a focus on profitable growth, Page Industries' stock price has compounded >30% CAGR, becoming >100x in the last 13 years and counting.

- *High switching costs*: This is synonymous with financial and/or psychological pain caused to customers when they switch to an alternate product or competitor. Imagine you are using all your business operations on Oracle's SAP software, and each datapoint around your processes is linked to a single software. What kind of business disruption will happen if it is suddenly shut or switched elsewhere?

[1]Saurabh Mukherjea, *The Unusual* Billionaires (Penguin Random House India, 2016)

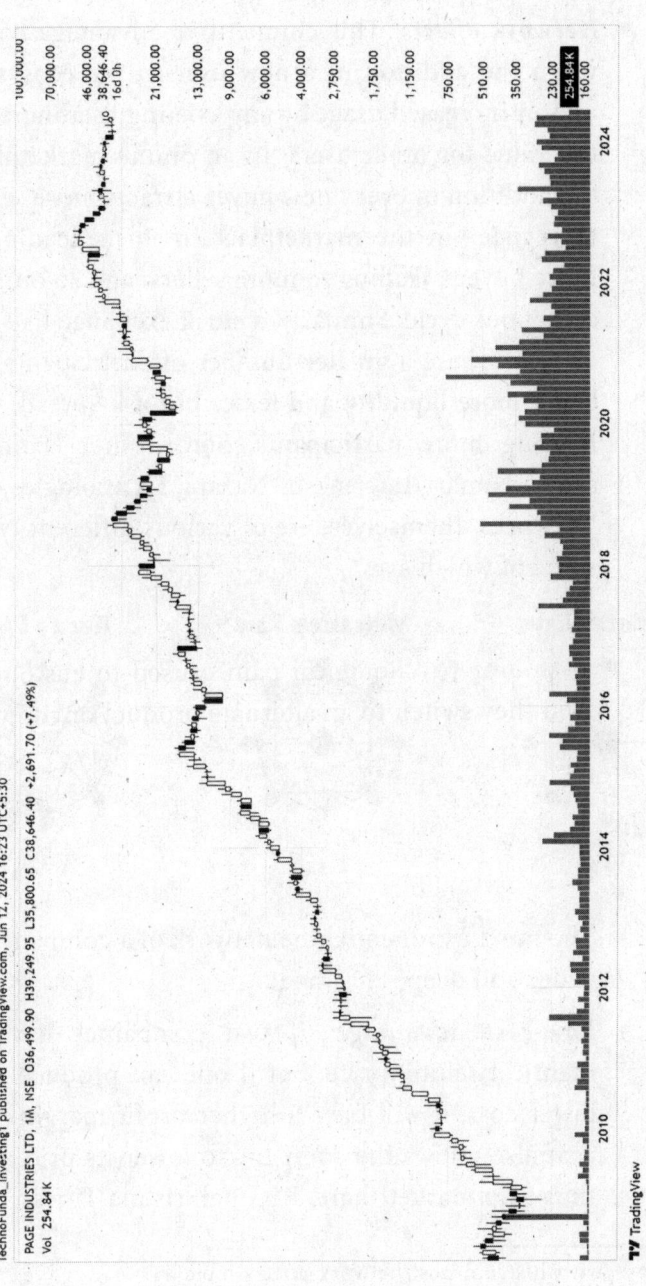

TechnoFunda_Investing1 published on TradingView.com, Jun 12, 2024 16:23 UTC-5:30

PAGE INDUSTRIES LTD, 1M, NSE O36,499.90 H39,249.95 L35,800.65 C38,646.40 -2,691.70 (-7.49%)

Vol 254.84K

- *Network effects*: This competitive advantage comes when the addition of a new user to the ecosystem and/or increased usage by any existing user increases the value for other users. In an online marketplace, the addition of every new buyer attracts more sellers to register in the marketplace, in turn, leading to more buyers, leading to more sellers, and so on, into a virtuous cycle. Similarly, a stock exchange like BSE or NSE where a greater number of participants will bring more liquidity and lesser bid-ask spread, thus inviting more participants. Some other examples are Indiamart Intermesh, Nazara Technologies, etc. Networks, themselves, are of various different types, some of which are:[2]

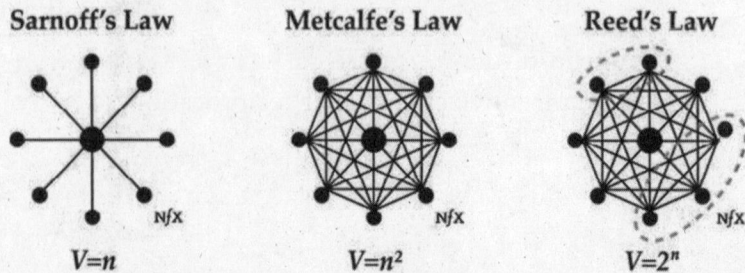

The more exponential the network of a company, the wider and deeper it's moat.

- *Low-cost advantage*: If two companies have an identical selling price, but if one can produce for a lower cost, it will have a higher profit margin. Low cost also allows the company to lower its prices and thus gain market share. E.g., Balkrishna Tyres.

---

[2]https://www.nfx.com/post/network-effects-bible

- *Economies of Scale*. Larger companies can produce more by spreading the cost of production over a larger amount of goods, leading to lower unit costs. E.g., ITC and Asian Paints. This moat is even more potent when the company passes on these lower unit costs to the customer, in the form of lower prices; Nicholas Sleep calls this scale economies shared. He writes- "Scale economics shared operations are quite different. As the firm grows in size, scale savings are given back to the customer in the form of lower prices. The customer then reciprocates by purchasing more goods, which provides greater scale for the retailer who passes on the new savings as well. Yippee. This is why firms such as Costco enjoy sales per foot of retailing space four times greater than run-of-the-mill supermarkets. Scale economics shared incentivizes customer reciprocation."[3]

- *Patents and IP*: E.g., L&T Technology Services has large numbers of patents of their own and co-filed with clients. Autoline Industries has a patent on certain aspects of the pedals and brakes of their 'E-Speed' electric cycle. Coke's syrup recipe and Nestle's Maggi masala are perfect examples of IP.

- *Strategic assets*: The relationship of the Genomals, promoters of Page Industries, with Jockey International, USA, is Page's biggest strategic asset. Jockey renewed its license with Page in 2010 for twenty-one years instead of five years, which was the

---

[3]https://igyfoundation.org.uk/wp-content/uploads/2021/03/Full_ Collection_Nomad_Letters_.pdf#page=151

earlier practice. Thus, until 2030, Page will remain Jockey's exclusive franchise in India and the UAE. Similarly, the relationship of Jubilant Foodworks with Domino's International is a very crucial strategic asset.

Moats are a way for companies to fight mean reversion, which is like a strong current in markets that pulls everything toward average. Michael Mauboussin has done some good work on **Measuring the Moat.**[4] He suggested an interesting mental model to find Moat in the sector value chain using an industry **map.**

This details all the players that touch an industry. For airlines, this would include aircraft lessors (such as Air Lease), manufacturers (Boeing), parts suppliers (B/E Aerospace) and more. Michael aims to show where the profit in an industry winds up. These profit pools can guide you on where you might focus your energies. For example, aircraft lessors make good returns; travel agents and freight forwarders make even-better returns.

Often, though, the most profitable investments occur when moats are in the making rather than after the moat is already established. Hence, one should consider companies that have relatively narrower moats, that are widening rather than already wide ones, which are stagnant.

There might be instances when companies are spending on R&D, Brand building, building distribution networks, trying to launch new products, trying to enter new markets,

---

[4]https://csinvesting.org/wp-content/uploads/2013/07/Measuring_the_Moat_July2013.pdf

spending heavily to gain economies of scale, or creating network effects, etc. Basically, they are bleeding today to achieve sustainable long-term growth. This is also known as short-term pain for long-term gain, and is a form of delayed gratification.

This reflects poorly on income statements in the short term, but the long-term owner earnings power of the company is constantly increasing, which results in exponential long-term growth.

EXAMPLES INCLUDE:

- Amazon hiring staff to increase future sales by making systems and servers more efficient
- Thyrocare taking a hit on the margins to quickly gain market share from lower prices and harness economies of scale in future
- Pharma companies expensing out their R&D costs rather than capitalizing on them

Also, due to the accounting principles in certain businesses, the earnings appear depressed. As Marcellus Investment Managers writes, "Indian life insurers are *not* allowed to amortise expenses incurred to acquire the customer over the life of the insurance policy. As a result, while the premium income is earned over a period, the customer acquisition expenses are debited to the P&L in the year of acquisition itself. Given that life insurance policies are long term in nature and extend to more than 20 years in many cases, upfronting of expenses for revenues which will be accrued over the next twenty years substantially understated accounting profitability of life insurers."[5]

Some indicators of companies in the value-chain having Moats:

- Pricing power
- Track record to earn a high return on invested capital
- High gross and operating margins for long periods of time

Pricing Power can be understood through the ability of a company to consistently raise prices at levels exceeding inflation. As Warren Buffett has further explained this aspect:

"The single most important decision in evaluating a business is pricing power. If you've got the power to raise prices without losing business to a competitor, you've got a very good business. And if you need to have a prayer session before raising the price by 10 percent, then you've got a terrible business."

Pricing power will also ultimately reflect a high return on capital employed coupled with high operating margins and an efficient working capital cycle.

A high return on invested capital signifies that competition is at bay and the company can consistently produce returns above the cost of capital.

---

[5]https://marcellus.in/newsletter/kings-of-capital/simplifying-life-insurance-and-why-we-hold-hdfc-life/

The Gross/Operating profit margin is a good indication of the price people will pay relative to the input costs required to provide the goods. It's a measure of value-added for the customer.

COMBINING IT WITH REINVESTMENT

Saber Capital Management, in their blog, has described the powerful concept of "Legacy Moats" and "Reinvestment Moats".

Most businesses with a durable competitive advantage belong in the Legacy Moat bucket, meaning the companies *earn strong returns on capital but do not have compelling opportunities to deploy incremental capital at similar rates.*[6]

These are essentially our Mango category of businesses. These businesses are of high quality due to legacy competitive advantages but struggle to deploy incremental capital at similar/high rates.

There is an even more elite category of quality businesses that classify as having a Reinvestment Moat. These businesses have all the advantages of a Legacy Moat, but also have *opportunities to deploy incremental capital at high rates.*[7]

These are essentially our Banyan category of businesses. Not only do they have strong competitive advantages but they keep reinvesting at high rates for future growth.

---

[6]**Saber Capital Management,** https://sabercapitalmgt.com/importance-of-roic-reinvestment-vs-legacy-moats/
[7]**Saber Capital Management,** https://sabercapitalmgt.com/importance-of-roic-reinvestment-vs-legacy-moats/

And the math of Total IRR generation, even if Banyan category (Reinvestment Moat) businesses are bought at higher multiples, is astonishing when held for a long time. This math of MEGA COMPOUNDING MACHINES is rarely understood by investors. Notice the difference it creates even if 10-year exit multiples are assumed to be the same. This is the power of compounding.[8]

	Reinvestment Corporation	Undervalued Corporation
Current Earnings Power	$100	$100
Beginning Multiple	20×	10×
Current Valuation	$2,000	$1,000
Percent of Earnings Reinvested	100%	50%
Returns on Retained Earnings	25%	10%
Cumulative Dividends[*]	$0	$629
Year-10 Earnings Power	$931	$163
Year-10 Multiple	15×	15×
Year-10 Valuation	$13,970	$2,443
Total IRR[**]	21.5%	13.6%
Multiple on Original Investment	7.0×	3.0×

Note: IRR = internal rate of return.
[*]Assumes all earnings not reinvested are distributed as dividends.
[**]Pretax IRR, factoring in tax rates, will only further the advantage of Reinvestment Corp.
Source: Saber Capital Management.

---

[8]**Saber Capital Management,** https://sabercapitalmgt.com/importance-of-roic-reinvestment-vs-legacy-moats/

CHAPTER SUMMARY

- In the value creation principle, companies create value by using investor capital to generate future cash flows at return rates that surpass the initial capital cost.

- The combination of growth and return on invested capital (ROIC) relative to its cost drives value.

- Companies can sustain strong growth and high ROIC only if they have a well-defined competitive advantage.

- According to Warren Buffett, great businesses must have an enduring "moat" protecting their ROIC.

- A competitive advantage is a business's ability to outperform the competition.

- The competitive advantage period (CAP) is the duration that a company generates returns on investment (ROI) exceeding its cost of capital.

- Only a moat can maintain a longer-than-average CAP.

- A strong brand is a moat; it restrains the competition and enhances pricing power, as seen in Page Industries operations.

- A moat has a high switching cost enough to cause psychological pain when replacing it with another brand.

- Network effects are another type of moat; value creation occurs when a customer is added to the ecosystem, as seen in the BSE or NSE.

- A low-cost advantage is another moat; it increases a company's profit margin when the market price rate is constant and enables it to increase its market share by lowering prices.

- Strategic assets like Page Industries' exclusive partnership with Jockey International, USA, are also moats; the alliance makes Page industries Jockey's sole franchise distributor in India and the UAE until 2030.

- Profitable investments occur when moats are in the making, not after establishment.

- Companies are the best moat indicators because they have narrow moats that are widening instead of broad and stagnant moats.

- One example of a moat in value chains is pricing power, which translates to high returns on capital.

- A company with the ability to raise prices at levels exceeding inflation without losing consumers has a pricing power moat.

- An enterprise with a durable competitive advantage is a legacy moat.

- Legacy cannot deploy incremental capital at similar rates to Reinvestment Moats, also legacy moats.

YOUR REFLECTIONS

(Reflect on what you have learned and pen down your thoughts)

_____

_____

_____

_____

_____

_____

_____

_____

_____

_____

_____

_____

_____

_____

_____

_____

_____

_____

CHAPTER TEN
HIGH QUALITY

"Return on capital employed is one of the most
important measures of corporate performance –
it is the profit return which the management earns
on the capital shareholders provide."[1]
—Terry Smith

A high-quality business is one that can sustain a high return on the capital employed and is consistent over long periods of time. Why so? When you select a bank to open a savings account, given the risk of bank fraud is equal, wouldn't you choose the one with the highest rate of interest? Somehow, in businesses, people talk about growth in earnings per share. Firstly, earnings per share differ from cash flow, but more importantly, it does not factor in the capital employed to generate those earnings or the return earned on it.

---

[1]Terry Smith, *Investing for Growth: How to make money by only buying the best companies in the world – An anthology of investment writing, 2010–20* (United Kingdom: Harriman House, 2020)

This is one of the most important parameters. If a company can continue to reinvest at high rates of return over long periods of time, the stock and earnings keep compounding, which gives an exponential effect.

In our earlier tree analogy, the top two quadrants, Mango and Banyan, represent high quality, while the bottom part, Cactus and Weeds, represent low quality. One should never touch bottom quadrants unless there is potential to become bamboo (transitioning possibility to high quality), or one is consciously betting on cyclical in satellite portfolio, i.e., Palm tree.

It's simply a play of probability - the more you are exposed to high quality, the higher the probability of success in the long run. Hence, the core portfolio should be majorly allocated to high-quality businesses.

According to Charlie Munger,

"Over the long term, it's hard for a stock to earn a much better return than the business which underlies it earns. If the business earns 6 percent on capital over 40 years and you hold it for those 40 years, you're not going to make much different than a 6 percent return even if you originally buy it at a huge discount. Conversely, if a business earns 18 percent on capital over 20 to 30 years, even if you pay an expensive looking price, you'll end up with a fine result."[2]

---

[2]Charlie Munger, *"A Lesson on Elementary, Worldly Wisdom as it Relates to Investment Management and Business,"* Farnam Street (blog) 1994, https://fs.blog/great-talks/a-lesson-on-worldly-wisdom/

Many investors just look at Earnings growth but miss an important complementary aspect of investing, i.e. Return on Capital Employed.

"Growth can enhance or diminish the value of a company – growing a business with inadequate returns is simply sending good money after bad. But when a company has superior returns on capital employed, and a source of growth that enables it to reinvest a substantial portion of those returns, the result is a compound growth in its value and share price over time. It is important to realize that this is over the long term."[3]

A company deploys capital in asset manufacturing facilities, generating cash flow and profits. The total capital deployed by the company consists of equity and long-term debt. RoCE is a metric that measures the efficiency of capital deployment for a company, calculated as EBIT divided by capital employed. The higher the RoCE, the better is the company's capital allocation. Any business that is not making a RoCE of 12-15% is earning below its cost of capital essentially. Most businesses that earn RoCE of less than 15%, become value traps. If the RoCE earned by a firm is less than its cost of capital, it cannot pay the capital providers for this limited resource. The business destroys value for the shareholders, as they would have earned a higher return on their capital had they invested it somewhere else.

---

[3] Terry Smith, *Investing for Growth: How to make money by only buying the best companies in the world – An anthology of investment writing, 2010–20* (United Kingdom: Harriman House, 2020)

CHAPTER SUMMARY

- A high-quality business consistently makes a high return on capital employed over long periods.

- Earnings per share, not to be confused with cash flow, measure business earnings growth.

- Earning per share does consider capital employed to produce those earnings, or the earned return.

- When a company sustains high rates of return on reinvestments for a long time, the stock and earnings keep compounding, giving it an exponential effect.

- An investor's portfolio should contain high-quality businesses because exposure to such enterprises increases the odds of success.

- The price of a company's stock reflects its rate of return; thus, the share never out-earns the rate of return.

- The Return on Capital Employed (RoCE) is a significant complementary investment aspect for earnings growth.

- Many investors concentrate on earning growth and overlook RoCE even though it is a better indicator of capital allocation.

- Growth impacts the value of a company.

- Investing in a business with low returns is akin to sending good money after bad money.

- Invest in companies with high returns on capital employed and growth because it permits reinvestment of a substantial portion of the returns, resulting in a compounding value and share price growth over time.

- ROCE is a metric that measures the efficiency of capital deployment for a company, calculated as EBIT divided by capital employed.

- A higher ROCE is indicative of better capital allocation.

- A business with a RoCE below 12% -15% earns below its cost of capital.

- Enterprises with a RoCE below 15% become value traps.

- When RoCE is below the cost of capital, a company will be unable to pay the capital provider.

- Businesses with a lower RoCE than the capital cost destroy value for shareholders; the shareholders would have earned a higher return on their capital had they invested in a firm with a higher RoCE.

YOUR REFLECTIONS

(Reflect on what you have learned and pen down your thoughts)

_____

_____

_____

_____

_____

_____

_____

_____

_____

_____

_____

_____

_____

_____

_____

CHAPTER ELEVEN

IMPROVEMENT

"A business should be viewed as an unfolding movie, not as a still photograph."
—*Warren Buffett*

Investing is all about delta, that is, the rate of change. A poorly run company with improvement may be preferred over a well-run company with deterioration.

IN MARGINS:

A company can improve operating margins and net profit margins by increasing pricing power, through innovative products, building efficiency and adding premium products. These improvements can result into excellent profit growth, either for a temporary period or for the long term if the changes are structural. One often-seen pattern in margin expansion is of the shift from trading to manufacturing; this has occurred in Raghav Productivity Enhancers and Trident

Texofab. It could also be due to a shift in product/segment mix, towards higher-margin areas, e.g., Goodluck India increasing its share of the higher-margin forgings. Another pattern in margin improvement is when the exports share rises; often, margins for the same product are higher in exports than in domestic sales. This is noticeable in Panama Petrochem and Ramkrishna Forgings.

IN CAPITAL ALLOCATION:

Promoters/CEOs have five basic options to allocate capital:

1. Invest in existing operations
2. Acquire other businesses
3. Pay dividends
4. Pay down debt
5. Buyback stock

Here are three basic ways to raise money:

1. Issue stock
2. Issue debt
3. Use the cash flow of the business

Five basic options to allocate capital:	Three basic ways to raise capital:
1. Invest in existing operations	1. Issue stock
2. Acquire other businesses	2. Issue debt
3. Pay dividends	3. Use the cash flow of the business
4. Pay down debt	
5. Buyback stock	

Collective toolkit for capital allocation decision which if used wisely can generate excellent results

This forms the collective toolkit for capital allocation decisions which, if used wisely, can generate excellent results for the company.

When companies demonstrate the ability of efficient capital allocation to create shareholder value, then it can get re-rated and further execution accelerates this. An example could be the divestment of non-core assets, e.g., Piramal Enterprises sold part of the Healthcare business to Abbott in 2010 when it was trading at a cash bargain, and now it has been rapidly re-rated due to efficient capital allocation.

Some companies have a stellar track record of successful acquisitions, e.g., Pidilite. They acquired Dr. Fixit, M Seal, Steelgrip and so on. It is not that all their acquisitions have succeeded. Even the best of companies do make mistakes. However, as we have observed in this book, if your mistakes are small and your gains are large, you can create a lot of value.

Another example of a successful acquisition is when SJS Enterprises had acquired Exotech Plastics in CY 2021 at a cost of Rs 64 Cr, and has been able to achieve improvement in margins due to synergies, cross-selling to existing customers, etc. Through the Exotech acquisition, they entered chrome-plated parts, and have a plant near Pune with a capacity of 29.5 million units. They continue to selectively assess inorganic opportunities. Snapshot from the prospectus:

Expand our business through strategic inorganic growth opportunities

Although we intend to continue to grow organically, we believe that inorganic growth opportunities in India or outside India may act as an enabler for growing our businesses. We intend to continue to evaluate, and selectively pursue, inorganic opportunities where products, resources, capabilities, operations and strategies are complementary and that will diversify our product portfolio, provide us access to a wider customer base, help us expand into new markets and geographies and consolidate our existing capabilities. These opportunities could be by way of strategic alliances, acquisitions, joint ventures, technological collaborations, partner tie-ups and other strategic and business combinations.

One key indicator of improvement in capital allocation is when a company divests/monetizes its non-core/idle assets, e.g.:

1. La Tim Metal & Industries has a land parcel in Khopoli-Pali area and they are monetising it by converting it into an industrial park

2. Cineline India is selling its windmills

3. Autoline Industries is creating an industrial park from its excess land

Interested readers can go through the recent concalls and the FY21 annual report of Mahindra & Mahindra to understand improvement in capital allocation through a live case study (as of the printing of this book in 2022). They are systematically categorizing loss-making subsidiaries, improving the cash flow position by lower fixed costs and working capital, etc.

IN DISCLOSURES/CORPORATE GOVERNANCE STANDARDS:

There are several instances where disclosures for many small and midcap stocks are minimal. Also, some of these companies are too small to form part of a mandate for large investors.

E.g., companies like Poddar Developers and Mold-Tek Packaging did QIPs (Qualified Institutional Placements), which resulted in higher disclosure and comfort from institutional shareholding.

Where governance improves, e.g., Mirza International, where there is a demerger of Indian business and corporate governance is improving, there is often a big re-rating factor. With Mirza, the company took loans from the bank. The promoters guaranteed that the company will pay the loans. For that guarantee, promoters charged a guarantee commission.

This was in FY 2016:[1]

6	Guarantee Commission		
	Mr. Irshad Mirza	163	37Cr.
	Mr. Rashid Ahmed Mirza	163	35Cr.
	Mr. Shahid Ahmad Mirza	163	35Cr.
	Mr. Tauseef Ahmad Mirza	163	36Cr.
	Mr. Tasneef Ahmad Mirza	163	33Cr.

Sl. No.	Particulars	Nature of Relationship	Volume of Transactions	Outstanding
	For the year ended March 31		2021	as on March 2021
6	Guarantee Commission			
	Mr. Rashid Ahmed Mirza	Key Management Personnel	0	0
	Mr. Shahid Ahmed Mirza	Key Management Personnel	75	0
	Mr. Tauseef Ahmed Mirza	Key Management Personnel	75	0
	Mr. Tasneef Ahmed Mirza	Key Management Personnel	75	0

In FY21, this got reduced to only 75 lakhs![2]

Corporate governance can also improve when there is a renewed focus in the management and dedication to

---

[1] https://www.bseindia.com/bseplus/AnnualReport/526642/5266420316.pdf#page=97
[2] https://www.bseindia.com/bseplus/AnnualReport/526642/70453526642.pdf#page=106

resolve previous poor governance activities, e.g., Tilaknagar Industries wanting to resolve auditor qualifications. From investor presentation:

Resolution of auditor qualifications

- Focus on taking proactive measures to resolve all auditor qualifications

(https://www.bseindia.com/xml-data/corpfiling/ AttachHis/75526b2b-553a-444e-b3b3-06e5c2691a9e. pdf#page=12)

It can also be due to new promoters, e.g., Burman group coming in as promoters in Eveready Industries; the previous promoters, Khaitan family, had several inter-corporate deposits etc.

CHAPTER SUMMARY

- According to Warren Buffett, businesses constantly evolve like a movie and are not stagnant like a photograph.

- Investing focuses on the rate of change or improvement.

- Even a poorly run company showing improvement is better than a well-managed business with decreasing value.

- The five basic options for capital allocation are investing in existing operations, acquiring other businesses, paying dividends, paying down debt, and buying back stock.

- The three basic ways to raise money include issuing back stock, issuing debt, and using the business's cash flow.

- When businesses utilize the capital allocation collective tool kit wisely, they can improve their results.

- Efficient capital allocation generates shareholder value and can become re-rated with continued efficiency.

- Companies with sustained capital allocation efficiency accelerate the re-rate execution function.

- Piramal Enterprises is an example of a company that achieved a rapid re-rate.

- Piramal Enterprises sold a section of its healthcare business to Abbott in 2010 when it was trading at a cash bargain.

- Currently, Piramal Enterprises is rapidly re-rated because of its efficient capital allocation.

- Even the best companies make mistakes— so long as the mishaps remain small and the gains great— there will still be shareholder value.

- Disclosures and corporate governance also influence shareholder value.

- However, the disclosure effect may be negligible for small companies.

- Nevertheless, companies like Poddar Developers and Mold-Tek Packaging did QIPs, which resulted in higher disclosure and comfort from institutional shareholding.

- An improvement in corporate governance boosts a company's re-rating factor.

- An example of corporate governance boosting the re-rated factor is Mirza International, where the demerger of the Indian business and corporate merger is improving.

- Mirza International took loans from the bank, and promoters guaranteed the company would pay the loan and charged a guarantee commission.

- Corporate governance can also improve when there is a renewed focus on the management and dedication to resolving past governance insufficiencies.

YOUR REFLECTIONS

(Reflect on what you have learned and pen down your thoughts)

_____

_____

_____

_____

_____

_____

_____

_____

_____

_____

_____

_____

_____

_____

_____

_____

_____

_____

CHAPTER TWELVE
NEW FACTOR

"Innovation distinguishes between a leader and a follower"
—Steve Jobs

Why new? Newness is the mantra of the modern world. Do you ever read old magazines? There is a reason the newspaper is called the **new**spaper. While the EMH is false and the market is never efficient all the time, it is efficient the majority of the time. Thus, for a large majority of the time, the market has factored in (hence 'priced in') old factors. Hence, as William O'Neil correctly writes, "It takes something new to produce a startling advance in the price of a stock."[1] Sales Growth generally comes from gaining market share in the existing markets, expanding into new markets and creating new products.

---

[1] William O'Neil, *How to make money in stocks* (New York: McGraw Hill, 2009)

What can be included under new?

New capacity: Companies doing a large CapEx could be potential opportunities, as earnings could potentially rise multi-fold post this. Generally, companies that double their capacity can be interesting, e.g.:

1. Fineotex Chemical recently did greenfield CapEx to take the total installed capacity to 79000 MTPA from the earlier 43000 MTPA, at a cost of ₹ 27 Cr.

2. Vidhi Specialty Food Ingredients.

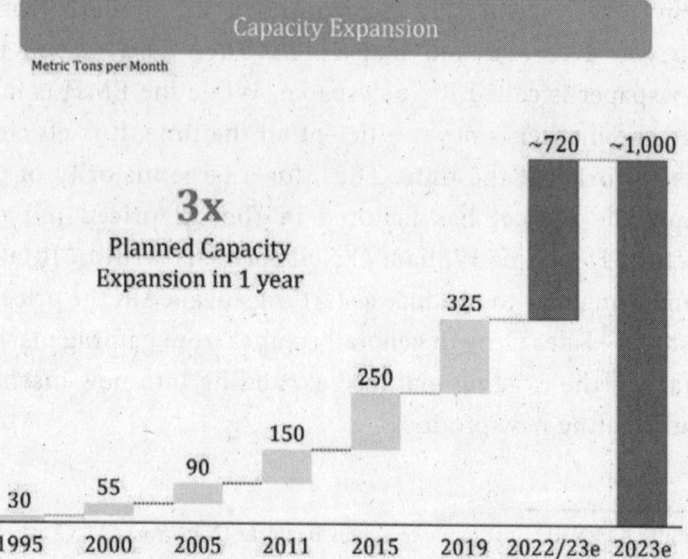

Existing Capacity of over

3,500 MT p.a.

+

~8,500 MT p.a. under expansion

Capacity Expansion

Metric Tons per Month

3x
Planned Capacity
Expansion in 1 year

30 — 1995
55 — 2000
90 — 2005
150 — 2011
250 — 2015
325 — 2019
~720 — 2022/23e
~1,000 — 2023e

3. Poddar Pigments is setting up a plant with an initial capacity of 5,000-6000 tonnes per annum, entailing a capital expenditure of ₹ 85 crores to be funded through internal cash accruals.

4. Raghav Productivity Enhancers is expanding its ramming mass manufacturing capacity from the existing 180,000 TPA to 288,000 TPA.

New product launch: Apple launched new products like the iPad, iPhone and so on, and these became major drivers of Apple's revenue growth. That leads to earnings growth, and ultimately stock prices are slaves of earnings growth. Also, new product launches help to diversify the company's revenue stream. For example, a company may be overly dependent on only one or two of its products, and any stagnation in the sales for these products can lead to poor growth for the company. Hence, a company that launches new products continuously adds new drivers for its growth, thus extending its growth period. This gets rewarded by the market in rising share prices.

Here are some examples of how Indian companies that launched new products created excellent returns for their shareholders:

1. Eicher Motors came out with Royal Enfield Classic 350 and 500 models in 2009, which changed the trajectory of the company. From its lows in 2009, the stock surged almost ~100x in the next 6 years, coupled with other successful new product launches like Thunderbird, Continental GT, etc.

2. Radico Khaitan rose after launching Magic Moments Dazzle Vodka and Royal Ranthambore Heritage Collection Royal Crafted Whisky.[2]

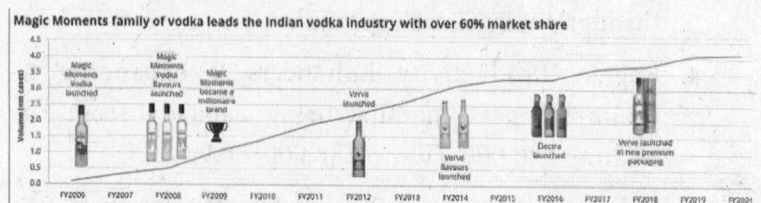

Magic Moments family of vodka leads the Indian vodka industry with over 60% market share

(Source: Company Disclosures)

3. Somany Home Innovation is launching IoT-enabled chimneys and stoves under the Hindware brand.

4. Amrutanjan launches roll-on balms and Comfy sanitary napkins.

5. Mahindra & Mahindra is launching several new automotive models.[3]

6. Autoline Industries has launched "E-Speed" electric cycles and is planning to launch electric scooters.

7. Raghav Productivity Enhancers is launching a new value-added boron oxide ramming mass.

8. Tilaknagar Industries is planning several new product launches in the coming quarters.

---

[2]https://www.business-standard.com/article/markets/radico-khaitan-rallies-11-after-launches-two-new-premium-imfl-121101200328_1.html
[3]https://www.mahindra.com/resources/investor-reports/FY21/Earnings%20Update/TRANSCRIPT-M-M-Annual-Analyst-Meet-28th-May-2021-FINAL.pdf

9. Inflame Appliances is planning the launch of dishwashers, oven-toaster-grill (OTG), etc. in the coming years.

New management/promoters: Let us continue with the kite analogy we have used. One of the most important factors is how good the kite flier (company management) is. Even if there are huge amounts of breeze enough to generate power through windmills, and the kite is optimally designed in its weight and structure, if you give it to someone who does not know how to fly a kite, what is the point? Often, there are instances of the next generation of promoters taking over the operations of the business and changing business strategy. Often, the next generation has a hunger, a 'fire in the belly' and large aspirations for business growth, which were not present in the older generation, who were 'content' with modest, mid-single-digit growth rates. When growth rates accelerate, a company can move from the Mango Tree to the Banyan Tree category, creating tremendous shareholder value. This is precisely what transpired in Lupin when Vinita Gupta took over. She played an instrumental role in taking Lupin beyond India and into the overseas markets. "If we did this in the US, we would be ten times the size, given the market potential," she would often tell her father, Desh Bandhu Gupta.[4]

There are several such examples where changes in top management played an instrumental role to take the company to a new trajectory:

---

[4]https://wow.outlookbusiness.com/vinita-gupta/

1. We covered new product launches by Eicher Motors and this was also the case of new management, i.e., Siddharth Lal as the think-tank behind the success story.

2. In 2013, Varun Berry joined Britannia Industry. Under Berry's watch, the company has doggedly pursued a strategy to improve its sales and distribution reach, better the overall cost management, increase its in-house production capabilities, infuse operational efficiencies across its supply chain and scale up its innovation capabilities.[5] The net profits surged almost ~4x between 2013-2018 and the stock price soared almost ~10x within the same period.

3. Mr. Shivaji Akhade replaced Mr. Umesh Chavan as CEO of Autoline Industries, and Mr. Venugopal Rao Pendyala (ex-Tata Motors) came in as CFO.

4. Panjri group bought Vistar Amar (earlier Shubhra Leasing) and the stock is up more than 15x in less than 7 years!

New Geography: Continuously expanding across new geographies can give a great scale for the company. We all know how multi-national companies like Pepsi and Coke have expanded into different countries to keep compounding in profit growth.

A classic case study in India is V-Guard Industries. It was having predominantly South India-based distribution with

---

[5]https://www.forbesindia.com/article/super-50-companies-2015/britannia-industries-the-taste-of-success/40701/1

95% revenue from the south and a mere 5% revenue from non-south (North India) back in 2008.

They adopted a long-term strategy to expand rapidly into a non-south distribution network. In 2012-13, non-south markets contributed ~25% of revenues. In FY21, they had ~42% of revenue from non-south markets.[6]

Due to this strategy, and other key initiatives, the profits of the company grew from ₹ 25 crores in FY 2010 to ₹ 200 crores in FY 2021

Distribution of Revenue	South	Non-South
FY2011	78%	22%
FY2012	79%	21%
FY2013	75%	25%
FY2014	70%	30%
FY2015	67%	33%
FY2016	67%	33%
FY2017	65%	35%
FY2018	63%	37%
FY2019	61%	39%
FY2020	60%	40%
FY2021	58%	42%

Source: Company Annual Reports and disclosures

[6]https://www.vguard.in/uploads/investor_relations/annual_report_2012_13.pdf

https://www.bseindia.com/bseplus/AnnualReport/532953/68929532953.pdf

Aptus Value Housing Finance India is planning to expand geographically and enter Maharashtra, Orissa and Chhatisgarh.

New price high of stock: Imagine the following: you buy a stock at ₹ 100. Where would you prefer the stock to go, ₹ 200 or ₹ 50? ₹ 200, right? Now consider this. How can the stock ever possibly go from ₹ 100 to ₹ 200? It must hit ₹ 110, ₹ 120, ₹ 130… and so on. In other words, it must create new highs! Most naïve investors try to look for stocks at or near their 52-week lows! It is important to note here that the time frame is crucial and must be adjusted depending on market conditions. During a strong, broad-based bull market rally, one should look for stocks making <u>multi-year</u> highs. But hardly any stocks will be making multi-year highs during a market crash. In such a scenario, one should look at stocks making one-month highs or quarterly highs. During a largely sideways market, 52-week (i.e., one year) highs are optimal. As Gautam Baid has aptly written, "A stock going to a new high is typically a bullish event, because the market has eliminated the supply of all previous buyers who experienced a loss and were waiting to get out at even. A stock hitting a new high has no overhead supply to contend with and has much more of an open running field. Everybody has a profit; everybody is happy. In contrast, a stock near its fifty-two-week low has a great deal of overhead supply to work through and lacks upside momentum, because it is vulnerable to fresh bouts of selling by the old investors at every higher level…The fifty-two-week high list is often a shortcut to the minds of smart investors."[7]

---

[7]Gautam Baid, *The Joys of Compounding* (New York, Columbia University

CHAPTER SUMMARY

- William O'Neil accurately stated, "It takes something new to produce a startling advance in the price of a stock."

- Sales grow when a business increases its market share in the existing market, ventures into new markets, and diversifies its product portfolio.

- Apple is a good example of how a new product launch can promote sales growth; when the company introduced the iPad, iPhone, and iPod, it increased its revenue generation, which, in turn, boosted its earnings growth and stock prices.

- Eicher motors increased its stock prices six years in a row after a low period when it introduced Royal Enfield Classic 350 and 500 models in 2009.

- A change in management is instrumental in catapulting a company's sales and increasing stock prices.

- A stock needs to create new price highs for long-term profitability.

- It is naïve investing to look for stocks experiencing a 52-week low.

- The investment time frame is vital and is modified depending on market conditions.

- During a strong-broad-based bull market rally, investors should look for stocks making multi-year highs.

Press, 2020)

- During a market crash, invest in stocks making one-month highs or quarterly highs.

- Highs are optimal in a largely sideways market in a 52-week time frame.

- According to Gautam Baid, when a stock goes through a new high, the event is typically bullish because previous buyers who experienced loss from the supply got eliminated.

- When a stock gets to a new high, it does not need to contend with overhead supply; the event resembles an open running field.

- Every investor profits when the stock hits a new high.

- On the other hand, a stock nearing a 52-week low has an overload of overhead supply to work through and lacks upside momentum because it is vulnerable to fresh bouts of selling by the old investors at every higher level.

- Smart investors regard 52-week high lists as shortcuts.

YOUR REFLECTIONS

(Reflect on what you have learned and pen down your thoughts)

_____

_____

_____

_____

_____

_____

_____

_____

_____

_____

_____

_____

_____

_____

_____

_____

_____

_____

CHAPTER THIRTEEN

EXECUTION OF EARNINGS GROWTH TRIGGERS

Steve Jobs said, "To me, ideas are worth nothing unless executed. They are just a multiplier. Execution is worth millions."[1]

The point is not to debate whether an idea is more important or execution. The point is that promoters often have a tendency of being overly optimistic about their business prospects. It may not necessarily be intentional to deceive potential shareholders; this may be purely due to excess optimism, which may not play out due to any external factors. Hence, it is important to not only look at what

---

[1]https://www.azquotes.com/quote/1059401

vision or guidance the management has given but also track whether they can execute it. As a part-owner of a business, one should look for management teams that actively walk the talk rather than over-promising and under-delivering.

CASE STUDY - RISE IN INDIAN TELECOM INDUSTRY

The period of 2003-2009 was probably a glorious one for the Indian Telecom Industry. The advent of competition later, like Tata DoCoMo, Videocon, Reliance Jio, etc. then made this sector highly competitive.

Let us now look at the comparison of MTNL vs. Bharti Airtel - both had sector tailwinds, megatrends in place, demand for their product, and competitive advantages. The execution of these earnings growth triggers made a huge difference. MTNL destroyed wealth vs. Bharti Airtel created enormous wealth for its shareholders.

All Number in INR Crores

MTNL	*Mar/2003*	*Mar/2009*
Net Sales	5,809	4,496
PAT	878	206
Market Cap	6,051	4,353

Bharti Airtel	*Mar/2003*	*Mar/2009*
Net Sales	3,050	37,352
PAT	176	8,044
Market Cap	5,245	1,18,792

The best way to track execution is to closely monitor the quarterly results. Like the weather has seasons- summer, monsoon, winter, spring, and autumn; investing has four seasons/quarters. These are the four quarters- Q1, Q2, Q3 and Q4. Closely tracking quarterly results can help an investor to identify the change in a company in the initial stages, for example, an increase in profit margins, increase in depreciation (which could be a signal of new CapEx being capitalized), decrease in interest cost (which could indicate that debt has been reduced), etc. One should also attend post-earnings conference calls. Often, many smart analysts attend these conference calls and ask questions that one could have never even imagined.

One of the most important patterns in investing is called post-earnings announcement drift (PEAD). It describes the drift of a firm's stock price in the direction of the firm's earnings surprise for an extended period. An earnings surprise does not lead to a full, instantaneous adjustment of stock prices, but a slow, predictable drift. It describes the tendency of stock prices to continue to behave as if the market participants were still anticipating the results, even though the results have been published and are widely known. This shows that studying quarterly results, even after they have been published, can yield great returns.

As Jesse Stine explains, "Asc is often the case, many investors will assume that a 'monster quarter' is a one-time event. Because of this thinking, investors don't initially bid the stock up in line with its newly improved fundamentals. While a substantial temporary disconnect exists between the stock price and the improved fundamentals, the astute investor is presented with an excellent low risk/high reward window of opportunity for entry."[2]

'Breakout earnings' where a company grows profit by more than 50% QoQ (Quarter on Quarter) and 300% YoY (Year on Year) for the quarter, are often an early indication of some structural change occurring. These can often be spotted using quantitative screeners on websites like screener.in

After the initial hyper and high growth phases, growth rates taper off to the mean rate (which is usually the nominal GDP growth rate). This is due to both competition and the company's own high-base effect. However, competent managements can delay such reversion to mean either by new streams of organic growth, and/or inorganic growth via judicious, earnings accretive and value-enhancing acquisitions.

---

[2]Jesse Stine, *Insider Buy Superstocks* (Superstock Letter, 2013, Page 89)

CHAPTER SUMMARY

- Steve Jobs aptly said, "Ideas are simply multipliers without execution because the latter is worth millions."

- As an investor, it is crucial to look beyond the vision or guidance provided by management by analyzing a company's proactiveness in executing.

- Business owners should look for management teams that walk the talk, not overpromising and under-delivering.

- In a case study of the highly competitive India's Telecom Industry, MTNL destroyed wealth, and Bharti Airtel created enormous wealth for its shareholders, despite both companies having tailwinds, megatrends, and product demand working in their favor.

- The case study shows the difference between the two companies in executing these earnings growth triggers.

- The best way to track execution is to monitor quarterly results closely.

- Closely tracking quarterly results enables investors to recognize changes in a company in the initial stages—an upsurge in profit margins or depreciation is indicative of the capitalization of a new CAPEX, and a decline in interest cost shows debt reduction.

- Investors should also attend conference calls to ask every imaginable question regarding their potential investment.

- There is a significant investing pattern called post-earnings announcement drift (PEAD).

- PEAD describes the drift of a firm's stock price in the direction of the firm's earnings surprise for an extended period.

- An earnings surprise does not lead to a complete and instantaneous adjustment of stock prices, but a slow, predictable drift.

- Earnings surprise defines the tendency of stock prices to act as if market participants were still anticipating results despite results publication and investor knowledge.

- Studying quarterly results even after their publication can yield great returns.

- Breakout earnings are an indication of ongoing structural changes.

- The first hyper and high growth phases always taper off to a mean rate, usually the nominal GDP growth rate, because of competition and a company's high-base effect.

- Competent management can delay the nominal GDP growth rate by new streams of organic growth and inorganic growth through careful earnings of accretive and value-enhancing acquisitions.

YOUR REFLECTIONS

(Reflect on what you have learned and pen down your thoughts)

_____

_____

_____

_____

_____

_____

_____

_____

_____

_____

_____

_____

_____

_____

_____

_____

_____

_____

_____

_____

CHAPTER FOURTEEN

BAMBOO INVESTING - THE SATELLITE PORTFOLIO PLAY

*"Experience tends to confirm a long-held notion
that being prepared, on a few occasions in a lifetime, to act
promptly in scale, in doing some simple and logical thing,
will often dramatically improve the financial results of that
lifetime. A few major opportunities, clearly recognizable as
such, will usually come to one who continuously searches
and waits, with a curious mind that loves diagnosis
involving multiple variables. And then all that is required
is a willingness to bet heavily when the odds are extremely
favorable, using resources available as a result of prudence
and patience in the past."*

—Charlie Munger

The title of the chapter is Bamboo Investing, however, let me first clarify that it's not about investing in bamboo trees. It's about mental models' ways of learning.

Before we get to the point, here is a small puzzle. Below are the share price charts of a few companies over a certain time. What is common between them?

COMPANY-1: SPECIALTY CHEMICAL COMPANY

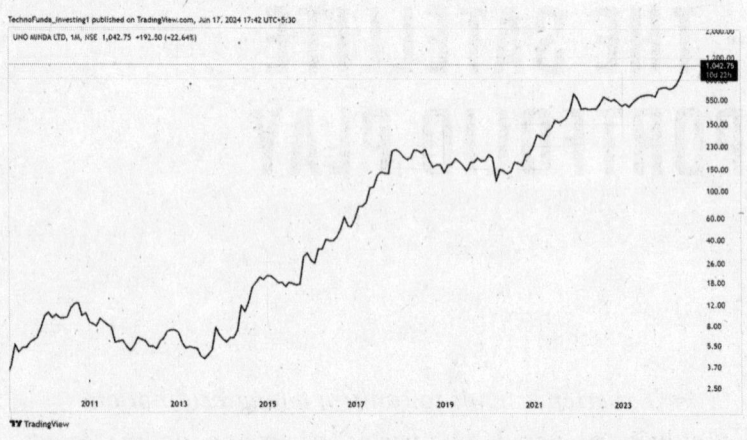

COMPANY-2: AUTO MANUFACTURING COMPANY

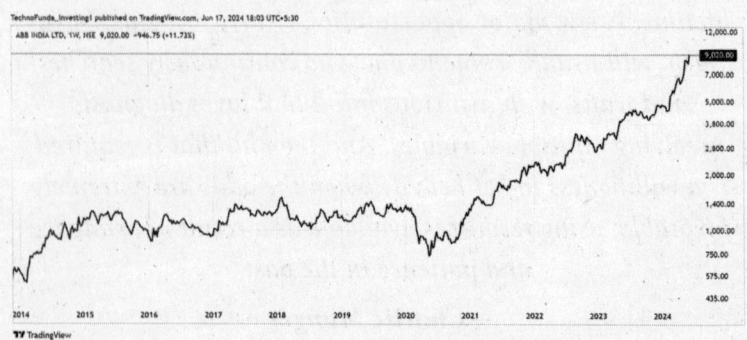

COMPANY-3: SHRIMP EXPORTING COMPANY

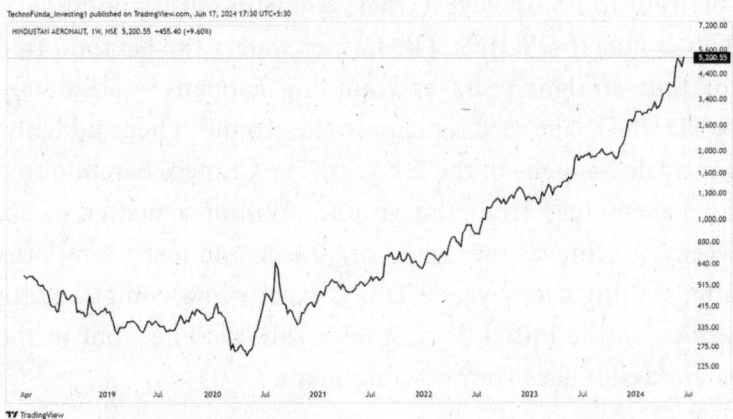

So, in this puzzle, there is another anecdote for you. This is about Chinese Bamboo. For those who haven't seen it, the picture is below. This will help you understand the Bamboo Investing concept.

The Chinese bamboo tree is very typical. It can grow vertically to almost 90 feet (that's almost as tall as a building!). *This is how it GROWS:* The farmer waters the bamboo tree for four straight years and nothing happens – absolutely NOTHING! The seed remains in the ground. Then suddenly, a miracle happens in the 5th year. The Chinese bamboo tree finally emerges from the ground. Within a matter of six weeks, it achieves the height of 90 feet....in just 1.5 months after waiting 4 long years! This is exactly how compounding works- in the initial days, it tests your patience, but in the later days, it tests your bewilderment.

LEARNING FROM THE STORY...

This is the common theme of the initial puzzle. A good stock may remain dormant and boring for many years, and then it would accelerate to surprise everyone. As such, this can happen for the entire sector or most stocks in any country, depending on triggers.

Therefore, one should watch for improvement in business fundamentals and Earnings power. If the prices don't move and the business is improving, that's the best ground to hunt.

So, the answer to the puzzle is that all the above companies were boring and dormant but accelerated to become multi-baggers in a very short period. The companies were Vinati Organics, Eicher Motors and Avanti feeds, but that's not important here.

What is imperative is, what are the triggers?

The above outcome is surprising as we say that markets are efficient. Then is there any anomaly?

Well, after a prolonged spell of research and rumination, I have found there are mainly two broad factors that drive it: Rapid earnings growth and PE re-rating (we have read about this in the core-satellite concept earlier).

1. SECTOR AND COUNTRY RE-RATING:

This can happen when there are certain key changes in the sector and country that can expand the PE multiple rapidly despite no change in earnings growth (mostly in anticipation of future earnings growth).

Examples:

- The entire Indian market got re-rated in 2014 after the new government got the majority in the elections
- PSU oil companies got re-rated due to deregulation of fuel prices
- Specialty chemicals and graphite electrode industry recently got re-rated due to the shutdown of factories in China

2. COMPANY IS WIDENING MOAT FOR THE LONG TERM:

There might be instances when companies are spending on R&D, brand building, building distribution networks, trying to launch new products, trying to enter new markets, spending heavily to gain economies of scale or creating network effects, etc. Basically, they are bleeding today to achieve sustainable long-term growth.

This reflects poorly on income statements for the short term, but the earnings power of the company is constantly increasing, which results in exponential long-term growth.

Examples:

- Amazon hiring staff to increase future sales by making systems and servers more efficient
- Thyrocare taking a hit on the margins to quickly gain market share from lower prices and harness economies of scale in future
- Ola/Paytm keeping 0% fees for partners (drivers/merchants) to achieve the network effect
- Tata Sky giving set-top boxes free/subsidized to new customers to bargain better with content providers in future

3. EFFICIENT CAPITAL ALLOCATION:

When companies demonstrate the ability of efficient capital allocation to create shareholder value, then it can get re-rated and further execution accelerates this.

EXAMPLES:

- Piramal enterprises sold part of its healthcare business to Abbott in 2010 when it was trading at cash bargain, and now it has been rapidly re-rated due to efficient capital allocation

4. INCREASED DISCLOSURE OR MARKET CAP LEVELS/ LOW LIQUIDITY:

There are several instances where disclosures for many small and mid-cap stocks are minimal. Also, some of these companies are too small to form part of the mandate for large investors.

There may be low liquidity for the stock. In these cases, the stock gets re-rated fast once it falls under the mandate of institutions or after improved disclosure levels.

Examples:

- Companies like Poddar Developers and Mold-Tek Packaging did a QIP, which resulted in higher disclosure and comfort from institutional shareholding
- Companies like Sirca Paints coming out from SME exchange and getting listed on BSE and NSE, thus constraint of many funds that cannot buy on SME platform gets removed

5. STRUCTURAL TURNAROUNDS:

Many companies could show lower earnings or losses due to some structural bottlenecks. But when this gets resolved, there may be a turnaround in the fortunes of the company.

This may be triggered due to single events like debt repayment, management change, regulatory change, change in strategy, consolidation of the industry, structural fall in raw material prices, etc.

Examples:

- Indo Count industries changed its strategy and product lines after coming out of BIFR and it became 100x in ~2-3 years thereafter
- Symphony changed its strategy from buying assets to becoming asset-light and its stock became a multi-bagger

- Autoline Industries is reducing debt, improving liquidity, entering EVs, reducing customer concentration, etc.

There may be several such factors that may result in multifold returns in a very short period. But not every company which is dormant or boring will move like this.

HOW TO IDENTIFY SUCH COMPANIES?

We can use the TechnoFunda approach, i.e., a combination of Technical and Fundamental analysis to find such Bamboo Investing stocks. Some of the technical indicators like price-volume break-outs, momentum indicators and formation of trend lines are very powerful in identifying such companies at an inflection point.

10 Powerful Indicators/Patterns for Investors

Sr. No.	Patterns/Indicators
1	Moving Averages
2	Parabolic SAR
3	Cup and Handle
4	Donchian Channels
5	ADX
6	Relative Strength
7	RSI
8	VStop
9	Channel Breakouts
10	ATR

You can research more on these indicators/patterns to understand how you can use them in your investing journey.

Adding fundamental analysis on top of it (remember the 4-cylinder analysis model) can filter some of the false signals generated by technical and helps to identify and ride such companies with conviction and then again technical analysis can be used to determine the Hold or Sell criteria.

Example:

Companies like BEPL, HEG, etc., gave clear technical indications and this was coupled with fundamentals like ABS prices going up along with CapEx for BEPL and graphite electrodes prices going up for HEG along with the shutdown of capacity in China.

See the technical chart below for HEG:

There was a price-volume break-out during Aug/Sep 2017 at ₹ 250-300 and the stock became almost 8x in less than 12 months. The fundamental news around the closing of the competitor came soon after the break-out, giving fundamental confirmation and conviction to hold. This was further accelerated by a shortage of supply in the market and promoter buying.

Do note, it is important to also have an exit strategy in place as it falls under cyclical stocks (Palm Tree stocks). More on the exit strategy in later chapters. For now, enjoy the Bamboo Investing process.

Thus, one must use the TechnoFunda approach to identify such stocks and once these are identified correctly, just SIT TIGHT until the story plays out and then average up to enjoy the Bamboo Investing way of wealth creation…!!

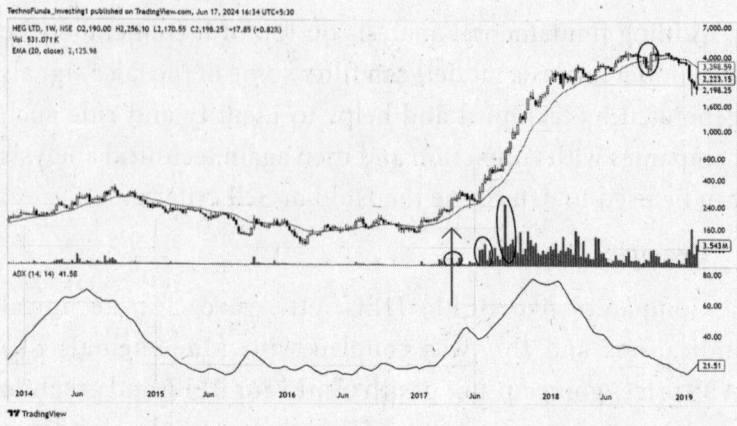

Bamboo stocks are not long-term investments. They generate alpha in portfolios in a short period of time, and you must exit them before the tide turns. The best way to exit them is to not get too greedy and keep some money on the table for the next buyer while strictly following your exit criteria.

CHAPTER SUMMARY

- A good stock remains dormant for years before it finally shoots up in price like a Chinese bamboo.

- Dormant stock can accelerate suddenly in any sector in a country with the right triggers.

- Investors should analyze business fundamentals and earnings power improvement; unchanged pricing indicates business improvement.

- Two broad factors trigger acceleration: rapid earnings growth and PE re-rating.

- Sector and country re-rating occurs when there are certain key changes in a sector and country expanding the PE multiple rapidly, even without changes in earnings growth.

- Exponential long-term growth is achievable by a company widening its moat; the company may experience short-term low-income statements as its earnings power continues to increase during this period.

- A business with efficient capital allocation creates shareholder value and gets re-rated; further execution accelerates this outcome.

- Minimal and numerous small and midcap stocks — for small businesses without large investor mandates— have low liquidity; such stock gets quickly re-rated when it falls under institutional mandates or after improved disclosure levels.

- Structural turnarounds also accelerate earnings growth; examples include debt repayment, management, regulatory and strategy changes, industry consolidation, structural fall in raw material prices, etc.

- Investors can identify businesses with earnings growth through technical indicators like price-volume breakouts, momentum indicators, and the formation of trend lines at their inflection point.

- Add fundamental analysis to filter false evaluations from technical indicators when identifying accelerating companies; together, the two identifying criteria make the TechFunda approach (from Technical and Fundamental analysis).

- Use the TechnoFunda approach to identify accelerating stock prices and wait until the prices average—this is the bamboo investing method of wealth creation.

- Bamboo stocks are a short-term investment strategy; they are significant for short-lived investment portfolios because investors must exit before the tide turns.

- The best way to exit is to practice contentment and leave some of the benefits for the next buyer; always abide by an exit strategy with bamboo stocks.

YOUR REFLECTIONS

(Reflect on what you have learned and pen down your thoughts)

_____

_____

_____

_____

_____

_____

_____

_____

_____

_____

_____

_____

_____

_____

_____

_____

_____

_____

_____

PART 3

REFINE

CHAPTER FIFTEEN

ALLOCATION AND POSITION SIZING

"It's not whether you're right or wrong that's important, but how much money you make when you're right and how much you lose when you're wrong"

—*George Soros*[1]

A common pattern among most successful investors across the world, be it Warren Buffett, George Soros, John Templeton, Rakesh Jhunjhunwala, Mohnish Pabrai, is that they allocate significant capital to their winners. When they are right - THEY BET BIG.

Most investors keep running behind the next big idea, that next big HDFC or next big Asian Paints, but they seldom think about allocation and position sizing. This is the most

---

[1]https://www.forbes.com/sites/bryanrich/2016/06/01/do-you-think-like-george-soros/?sh=77938a555f0d

under-appreciated idea in investing. I am sure all of us, in our journey, would have bought HDFC Bank or Astral Poly or Pidilite or Asian Paints, etc., but why did it not create similar wealth as other successful investors? The first factor is Riding Winners, and the second and most important is riding them by allocating big capital behind them.

No matter how well you may know your stocks, every business has unknown risks. The only way to protect against such risks is to diversify. What is the optimum number of stocks one should hold in a portfolio?

A portfolio of 15-20 stocks offers the best of both worlds – adequate diversification and a meaningful allocation to move the needle.

The graph below shows that somewhere around 19 stocks are the 'sweet spot' where most of the benefits of diversification are achieved. Adding more stocks beyond that is suboptimal.

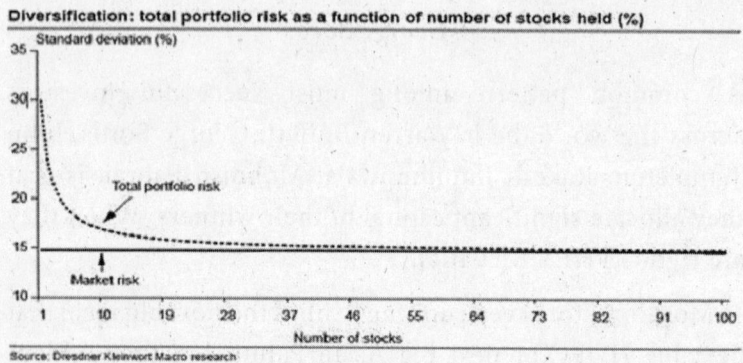

Diversification: total portfolio risk as a function of number of stocks held (%)

Source: Dresdner Kleinwort Macro research

Now let's understand the allocation part and how one can ride winners. In the below example, we have assumed a portfolio of 20 companies (to first have reasonable diversification in place). Now an important aspect of allocation plays a key role to determine portfolio returns.

Let's understand that Investing is a game of probability. We must always think in terms of "expected value". As Warren Buffett mentioned, "Take the probability of loss times the amount of possible loss from the probability of gain times the amount of possible gain. That is what we're trying to do. It's imperfect, but that's what it's all about."

As Anurag Sharma rightly explains in his masterpiece *Book of Value* - "Make no mistake: both gambling and investing are about making decisions now for outcomes in the unknown future. As such, they both require making assessments about the odds; understanding the underlying math is essential in either case. The difference is that where gamblers usually seek low odds with a high payoff , investors are inclined to seek out much more favorable odds for reasonably good returns (say, 9–1 odds for a 15 percent return with much upside potential). Marginally favorable odds (say, 51–49) would induce eager action from gamblers but none from investors."

No matter how good we are at stock selection and understanding businesses, we will only know in hindsight that any investment had a good or bad outcome. We will only know the odds or probability of winning. So how to naturally allocate more to winners and how to reduce allocation to non-performers?

The ideal strategy is to keep AVERAGING UP the businesses that keep performing and TRIM the ones not performing. This can fetch returns to your outstanding portfolio. Take a small initial allocation and then follow a pyramiding strategy.

Let me caution you that Averaging up is mentally very difficult due to Anchoring bias. Our mind gets fixated on the initial price even though a business might have improved significantly to justify the higher price.

"As soon as our intuition gets fixated with a number—and that can be any number—it sticks with us. Most of our decision-making errors result from mental shortcuts that are a normal part of the way we think. The brain uses mental shortcuts to simplify the very complex tasks of information processing and decision-making. Anchoring is the psychologist's term for one shortcut the brain uses. The brain approaches complex problems by selecting an initial reference point (the anchor) and making small changes as additional information is received and processed."

—Vishal Khandelwal

But if you can get rid of your own Anchoring bias and understand this math, it can give excellent portfolio returns that can help you accelerate your journey to achieve financial freedom and wealth creation.

The example below can give you an idea of it.

Here is how your portfolio returns will shape up based on various allocation strategies.

	Return (%)	Allocation to Stocks			Portfolio Returns		
		Portfolio A	Portfolio B	Portfolio C	Portfolio A	Portfolio B	Portfolio C
Company 1	100%	5%	15%	1%	5.0%	15.0%	1.0%
Company 2	90%	5%	15%	1%	4.5%	13.5%	0.9%
Company 3	80%	5%	10%	1%	4.0%	8.0%	0.8%
Company 4	70%	5%	10%	1%	3.5%	7.0%	0.7%
Company 5	60%	5%	8%	1%	3.0%	4.8%	0.6%
Company 6	50%	5%	8%	2%	2.5%	4.0%	1.0%
Company 7	40%	5%	6%	2%	2.0%	2.4%	0.8%
Company 8	30%	5%	6%	2%	1.5%	1.8%	0.6%
Company 9	20%	5%	4%	2%	1.0%	0.8%	0.4%
Company 10	10%	5%	3%	2%	0.5%	0.3%	0.2%
Company 11	0%	5%	2%	3%	0.0%	0.0%	0.0%
Company 12	-10%	5%	2%	4%	-0.5%	-0.2%	-0.4%
Company 13	-20%	5%	2%	6%	-1.0%	-0.4%	-1.2%
Company 14	-30%	5%	2%	6%	-1.5%	-0.6%	-1.8%
Company 15	-40%	5%	2%	8%	-2.0%	-0.8%	-3.2%
Company 16	-50%	5%	1%	8%	-2.5%	-0.5%	-4.0%
Company 17	-60%	5%	1%	10%	-3.0%	-0.6%	-6.0%
Company 18	-70%	5%	1%	10%	-3.5%	-0.7%	-7.0%
Company 19	-80%	5%	1%	15%	-4.0%	-0.8%	-12.0%
Company 20	-90%	5%	1%	15%	-4.5%	-0.9%	-13.5%
Total of Portfolio		100%	100%	100%	5.0%	52.1%	-42.1%

Portfolio A is an equal-weight strategy.[2]

The ideal way to add a position is through tranches. Charlie Munger has said, "To get what you want, you have to deserve what you want."[3]

Similarly, the stocks that eventually form 10, 15 or 20% of your portfolio should **deserve** that weight. And how do stocks *deserve* a large allocation? By earning it through price appreciation.

Diversification is not only about the number of stocks, but also about the correlation between stocks. This includes the geographical risk- your portfolio companies should not all be based in the same location, as any natural calamity like floods,

[2]https://www.investopedia.com/articles/stocks/11/illusion-of-diversification.asp

[3]https://www.goodreads.com/quotes/1399571-to-get-what-you-want-you-have-to-deserve-what#:~:text=Quotes%20%3E%20Quotable%20Quote-,%E2%80%9CTo%20get%20what%20you%20want%2C%20you%20have%20to%20deserve%20what,undeserving%20people.%E2%80%9D

earthquakes, etc. could be a problem. It also involves macro factors. As Gautam Baid writes in *The Joys of Compounding*, "Sometimes, factors like currency depreciation or rising interest rates hurt some of our portfolio companies while benefiting others, so that the overall impact is muted. Most notably, if we invest in a diversified portfolio of good businesses, then the tailwinds pushing a few businesses forward most of the time will compensate for the headwinds pushing back the others, thus protecting us from permanent loss of capital."

HOW TO SIZE THESE BETS?

There is very little academic study done on this aspect, but the best and closest which I have found was by John L. Kelly called "The Kelly Criterion". It is a mathematical formula that gives you output on Capital to Bet given win-loss probabilities and payoffs (odds).

The following appeared in Ed Thorp's interview in the book *Hedge Fund Market Wizards*:

$$F = Pw - (P_L / [\$W / \$L])$$

Where,

$\qquad$ F = Kelly criterion fraction of capital to bet

$\qquad$ Pw = probability of winning the bet

$\qquad$ P_L = probability of losing the bet

$\qquad$ $\$W$ = dollars won if the bet is won, and

$\qquad$ $\$L$ = dollars lost if the bet is lost[4]

---

[4]Jack Schwager, *Hedge Fund Market Wizards: How Winning Traders Win* (Hoboken, NJ; Wiley, 2012)

Let's understand $W / $L >>. It is basically a payoff, or what is commonly known as a Reward for the Risk Taken. Let's take the example of tossing the coin. Let's say you bet on either side and you are offered twice the reward if you are right. Then $W / $L becomes 2:1, so if you bet ₹ 500 and you are right, then you get ₹ 1000.

Pw and P_L are 50% each with tossing the coin. But when you are investing, it will depend on the probability of positive outcomes in your investment thesis, and similarly, the probability of downside risk materializing.

If we are just following the fundamentals, it becomes quite a tough exercise, but still, we can come to a reasonable estimate, given we understand the business well. If you use objective trailing exits and upside targets based on earnings and re-rating estimates, it becomes slightly easier.

Let's say we had a 75% probability of winning (basically, it is a high conviction idea in terms of investment thesis) and we were also having favorable entry conditions (in terms of valuation and market condition) with 5:1 reward:risk. Here 25% is the probability of losing.

Applying Kelly's formula with starting capital of ₹10,000, the bet size would be:

F = 75% - (25% / 5), i.e. 70% of capital, i.e. ₹ 7,000

Another example with a winning probability of 50% and 2:1 reward:risk would mean,

F = 50% - (50% / 2), i.e. 25% of capital, i.e. ₹ 2,500

In his book, *The Mathematics of Gambling,* Thorp explains the Kelly system's attractive features:[5]

1. The chance of ruin is "small". Because the Kelly system is based on proportional bets, losing all your capital is theoretically impossible (assuming money is infinitely divisible). A small chance of a significant drawdown remains.

2. The Kelly system is highly likely to grow a bankroll faster than other systems. Provided comparably attractive opportunities continue to appear, there is a high probability the system will generate a bankroll that exceeds other systems by a determinable multiple.

3. You reach a specified level of winnings in the least average time. If you have a financial end goal in mind and continuous opportunities, the Kelly system will likely allow you to achieve the objective in a shorter time than other systems.

You can also decrease volatility using the "half-Kelly." This means that if the formula suggests you put 30 percent of your bankroll in one stock, you put half of it (15 percent).

William Poundstone writes about half-Kelly: "This is an appealing trade-off because it cuts volatility drastically while decreasing the return by only a quarter. In a gamble or investment where wealth compounds 10 percent per time unit with full-Kelly betting, it compounds 7.5 percent with half-Kelly. The gut-wrenching and teeth-gnashing are

---

[5]Edward O. Thorp, *The Mathematics of Gambling* (Hollywood, CA: Gambling Times, 1984)

diminished much more. It can be shown that the full Kelly bettor stands a 1/3 chance of halving her bankroll before she doubles it. The half-Kelly bettor has only a 1/9 chance of losing half her money before doubling it."[6] [7]

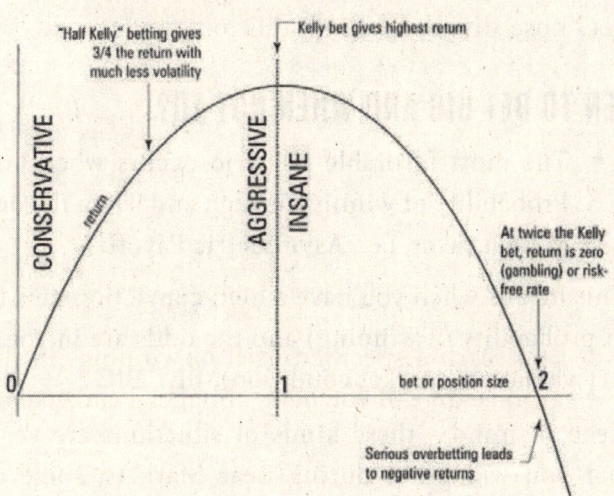

Aggressive vs. Insane Risk-Taking

The horizontal axis is the multiple (or fraction) of the Kelly Criterion applied; zero is betting nothing at all, and two is twice the Kelly bet. The vertical axis is the total compounded return. If one is looking only for the highest rate of return in the shortest period, then following Kelly Criterion is the best method for bet sizing.

In the mid-1960s, Buffett allocated close to one-quarter of his assets into one stock, American Express, when he

[6]William Poundstone, *Fortune's Formula: The Untold Story of the Scientific Betting System That Beat the Casinos and Wall Street* (Hill & Wang, 2005)
[7]William Poundstone, *Fortune's Formula: The Untold Story of the Scientific Betting System That Beat the Casinos and Wall Street* (Hill & Wang, 2005)

was convinced that the security offered superior return prospects.[8]

Ranjita: But how to gauge when to bet big and when to abstain? Is there a cut-and-dried technique?

Aryan: Bravo Ranjita, I admire your acumen.

Let's nose-dive deeper into this topic.

WHEN TO BET BIG AND WHEN NOT TO?

- The most favorable scenario occurs when both the Probability of winning is high and when the odds are in your favor, i.e., Asymmetric Payoff.

This means when you have a high conviction idea (with a high probability of winning) and the odds are in your favor (entry valuation, market condition), BET BIG

Keep in mind - these kinds of situations are very rare. Either you will get it during Bear Markets, some market anomaly or some special situations.

As Mohnish Pabrai in his book The Dhandho Investor mentions, "You need to take such - "Few Bets, Big Bets, Infrequent Bets" to make it big."

- When you have a low conviction idea with a low probability of winning but with high payoffs, BET moderately
- When you have lesser probability and low reward:risk, don't BET

---

[8]Roger Lowenstein, *Buffett: The Making of an American Capitalist* (Random House, 1995)

Also, remember that subsequent bets are a function of winning the first bet as the overall capital increases. If we think in the context of averaging up, it implies that if the probability of winning keeps increasing as the business performs and the price responds together, we need to keep adding capital.

Similarly, during the investing journey, if the probability of losing starts increasing due to risks in the business materializing and the reward-risk deteriorates, we need to keep trimming our positions.

For long enough bets, this overall strategy will maximize portfolio returns.

That's exactly the table in the example proved mathematically:

Portfolio A - we do not give attention to position sizing and give 5% capital to each of the 20 businesses and portfolio returns are 5%

Portfolio B - we average-up winners and give more allocation to winners and much less to losing bets and portfolio returns are a whooping 52%

Portfolio C - we average down and keep buying losing businesses with low reward:risk (reverse of Kelly formula) and the portfolio returns are pathetic negative 42%

Raamdeo Agrawal rightly mentioned his key lesson in the market:

"A significant learning was to average up - we used to make one-shot investments. If the research is good, one should average up. Now there is wisdom and experience.

Companies have their own life, and success breeds success. Now I am an entrepreneur as well and I am talking from my business experience. I run a slightly diversified company, not a monoline business. When you start a business, you struggle for five to ten years, and then you develop some competitive advantage and pick up. You won't know how big a success you can become. Even Hero Honda did not know that they could move from 12-13% to 55-60% market share. Clearly, it is very difficult to discover all the successes in advance."[9]

IMPORTANCE OF EDGE

One more variation of Kelly's formula is found in the book *Fortune's Formula* by William Poundstone, i.e.

F = edge/odds

F = Kelly criterion fraction of capital to bet

Edge = Expected value of the financial proposition

Odds = How much you win if you win

Now, let's understand this with the same coin-tossing example. We discussed a 50% probability of each winning and losing (as it's a fair coin). But the Odds or Payoffs were in our favor. If we win it is 2x and if we lose it is 1x.

F = (50%*2 - 50%*1) / 2 = 25% (one should put 25% of total capital in one bet)

For investing, generally, the key edge is the information edge, and the other is the analytical edge. As most investors

[9]Vishal Mittal and Saurabh Basrar, *Masterclass with Super-Investors -Raamdeo Agrawal Interview* (New Delhi: Maple Press India, 2018)

follow only fundamental analysis and markets are becoming more and more efficient - there is hardly any edge.

When you blend fundamentals and technicals (along with price volume action), it gives you an information edge as most times price volume action reflects fundamentals much ahead of information distribution in public.

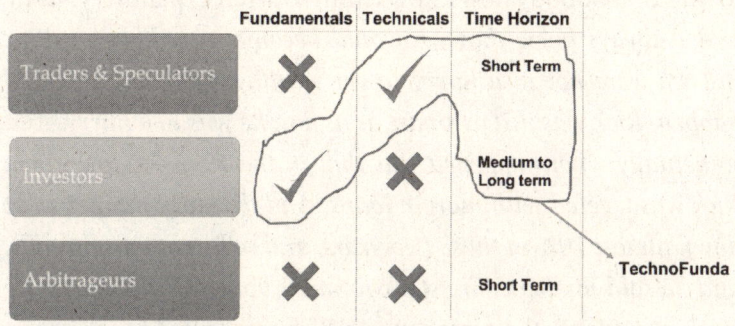

FOCUS ON THE RISK OF RUIN:

Who is the person on the rightmost? Everybody would know- Charlie Munger. Who is the person on the leftmost? Many would know- Mohnish Pabrai. But who is the person in the middle? Hardly anybody knows him. He is Rick Guerin.

Let us hear the story of Rick Guerin, who was Warren Buffett's and Charlie Munger's partner in the 1970s. But what happened to him that nobody now knows him? Warren explains, "*Charlie and I always knew that we would become incredibly wealthy. But we were not in a hurry to get wealthy; we knew it would happen. Rick was just as smart as us, but he was in a hurry. And so actually what happened was that in the 1973-74 downturn, Rick was levered with margin loans. And the stock market went down almost 70% in those two years, and so he got margin calls, and he sold his Berkshire stock to me. I bought Rick's Berkshire stock at under $40 a piece, and so Rick was forced to sell shares at … $40 apiece because he was levered.*"[10]

Guess what is the share price of Berkshire Hathaway today? Over $400,000! Charlie, Warren, and Rick were equally skilled at getting wealthy. But Warren and Charlie knew how to stay wealthy.

Gautam Baid writes, "Whenever someone sells in desperation, they tend to sell cheap. As a buyer, I love to be on the opposite side of such trades in which the other party is being forced to liquidate holdings at any price, regardless of underlying value. The time to buy is when those investors are in a hurry to dump shares at any price."[11]

---

[10]"To Get Rich, Don't Be a Rick". Safarl Niveshak, December 13, 2021. https://www.safalniveshak.com/dont-be-a-rick/

[11]Gautam Baid, *The Joys of Compounding* (New York, Columbia University Press, 2020)

If someone asks you to play tossing the coin game. You know that the probability of winning is 50% and losing is 50%. And you are told that bet size is compulsory ₹ 10 lakh. If you win, you get ₹ 1 crore, and you can lose ₹ 10 lakh. The payoff is 10:1. Will you play this game?

Mathematically, it may look very tempting and a no-brainer to play, but what if you have only ₹ 10 lakh capital? It means there is a RISK OF RUIN if you lose. So, here is what I strongly recommend; never play such a game that takes you out of the game, particularly in the game of investing.

As Rick Mears said- "To finish first you must first finish."[12]

Nassim Taleb says- "Rationality is avoidance of systemic ruin."[13]

In Investing, we also need to focus on consequences, not just probabilities.

Never leverage. As Buffett said: "If you're smart, you don't need leverage; if you're dumb, it will ruin you."[14]

Morgan Housel writes- "**The road to financial regret is paved with debt...** It's amazing what percentage of financial problems are caused by borrowing. Debt is a claim on your future, which you'll always miss, to gain something today, which you'll quickly get used to... Most debt is the equivalent

[12]https://www.passiton.com/inspirational-quotes/6447-to-finish-first-you-must-first-finish

[13]https://www.economist.com/books-and-arts/2018/02/22/nassim-taleb-explains-the-power-of-skin-in-the-game

[14]https://www.dividendgrowthinvestor.com/2021/04/warren-buffett-and-charlie-munger-on.html#:~:text=%E2%80%9CIf%20you're%20smart%20you,you%20double%20your%20net%20worth

of a drug: A quick (and expensive) hit of pleasure that wears off, only to drag you down for years to come, limiting your options while weighed down by the baggage of your past."[15]

True, no leverage may give you lower returns. But are returns more important than a good night's sleep? Buffett writes, "Our aversion to leverage has dampened our returns over the years. But Charlie and I sleep well. Both of us believe it is insane to risk what you have and need to obtain what you don't need."[16]

The risk of being multiplied by zero is too big a risk for a few percentage points of better returns. Buffett writes, "Unquestionably, some people have become very rich using borrowed money. However, that's also been a way to get very poor. When leverage works, it magnifies your gains. Your spouse thinks you're clever, and your neighbors get envious. But leverage is addictive. Once having profited from its wonders, very few people retreat to more conservative practices. And as we all learned in third grade—and some relearned in 2008—any series of positive numbers, however impressive the numbers may be, evaporates when multiplied by a single zero. History tells us that leverage all too often produces zeroes, even when it is employed by very smart people."[17]

Never bet too much, it wipes you down if you are wrong. And in markets, the best-laid plans of mice and men go

---

[15]https://www.fool.com/investing/general/2015/10/13/financial-advice-for-my-new-son.aspx
[16]Warren Buffett, *Berkshire Hathaway 2017 Annual Letter to Shareholders*, https://www.berkshirehathaway.com/letters/2017ltr.pdf#page=3
[17]Warren Buffett, *Berkshire Hathaway 2010 Annual Letter to Shareholders*, 2010, http://www.berkshirehathaway.com/letters/2010ltr.pdf

astray. No matter how much conviction we might have, things can get ugly.

"In almost every case of catastrophic failure that we've observed, we believe the root cause can ultimately be boiled down to one or a combination of just five factors. The five factors are 1) leverage 2) excessive concentration 3) excessive correlation 4) illiquidity and 5) capital flight."

—Zeke Ashton[18]

"In addition to magnifying losses as well as gains, leverage carries an extra risk on the downside that isn't offset by accompanying upside: the risk of ruin."

—Howard Marks[19]

Portfolio Loss	Gain Required to Breakeven
-10%	11%
-20%	25%
-30%	43%
-40%	67%
-50%	100%
-60%	150%
-70%	233%
-80%	400%
-90%	900%
-97%	3,233%

"Whenever a really bright person who has a lot of money goes broke, it's because of leverage."

—Warren Buffett

---

[18]http://mastersinvest.com/leveragequotes
[19]http://mastersinvest.com/leveragequotes

Morgan Housel has written:

"Getting money is one thing. Keeping it is another. If I had to summarize money success in a single word it would be "survival... The ability to stick around for a long time, without wiping out or being forced to give up, is what makes the biggest difference. This should be the cornerstone of your strategy, whether it's in investing, your career or a business you own. There are two reasons why a survival mentality is so key with money. One is obvious: few gains are so great that they're worth wiping yourself out over. The other... is the counterintuitive math of compounding. Compounding only works if you can give an asset years and years to grow. It's like planting oak trees: A year of growth will never show much progress, 10 years can make a meaningful difference, and 50 years can create something extraordinary. But getting and keeping that extraordinary growth requires surviving all the unpredictable ups and downs that everyone inevitably experiences over time. We can spend years trying to figure out how Buffett achieved his investment returns: how he found the best companies, the cheapest stocks, the best managers. That's hard. But equally important is pointing out what he didn't do. He didn't get carried away with debt. He didn't panic and sell during the 14 recessions he's lived through. He didn't sully his business reputation. He didn't attach himself to one strategy, one worldview, or one passing trend. He didn't rely on others' money (managing investments through a public company meant investors couldn't withdraw their capital). He didn't burn himself out and quit or retire. He survived. Survival gave him longevity. And longevity—investing consistently from age 10 to at least age 89—is what made compounding work wonders. That single point is what matters most when describing his success."[20]

In a way, the risk of ruin is the risk of starting over. It is the risk of going back to square one.

Buffett writes, "Charlie and I have no interest in any activity that could pose the slightest threat to Berkshire's wellbeing. (With our having a combined age of 167, starting over is not on our bucket list.) We are forever conscious of the fact that you, our partners, have entrusted us with what in many cases is a major portion of your savings. In addition, important philanthropy is dependent on our prudence. Finally, many disabled victims of accidents caused by our insureds are counting on us to deliver sums payable decades from now. It would be irresponsible for us to risk what all these constituencies need just to pursue a few points of extra return."[21]

Further, not only does survival protect your downside, but it could also expand your upside! If you survive, you can invest while everyone else is wiped out.

"By being so cautious in respect to leverage, we penalize our returns by a minor amount. Having loads of liquidity, though, lets us sleep well. Moreover, during the episodes of financial chaos that occasionally erupt in our economy, we will be equipped both financially and emotionally to play offense while others scramble for survival. That's

---

[20]Morgan Housel, *The Psychology of Money: Timeless Lessons on Wealth, Greed, and Happiness* (United Kingdom: Harriman House, 2020)
[21]https://jameslau88.com/2020/05/13/warren-buffett-on-debt-or-leverage/

what allowed us to invest $15.6 billion in 25 days of panic following the Lehman bankruptcy in 2008."[22]

In businesses, too, the risk of ruin is present. It is called fragility.

Chatur: Ahaa, this is a new term for me. What are sources of fragility?

Aryan: Well, there are a few triggers of fragility, let's review them one by one.

Lack of entry barriers: Lack of entry barriers causes fragility in the business in a way that the business loses its competitive advantage, e.g.: Go PRO

Businesses, where both input and output are commodities, are susceptible to fragility.

Disruption through innovation, e.g.: Nokia, Blackberry, Kodak.

Dependence on one or few customers, dependence on one or few suppliers, dependence on government subsidies. Dependence on the kindness of others can be a major source of fragility in the business.

Vulnerability to the price of something that is volatile and beyond control can bring out the fragility in the business, e.g., Titan when it was purchasing gold (before the gold-leasing model was adopted).

Rigid cost structures. High operating leverage cuts both ways: it is a double-edged sword. Gambling tendencies by managers can bring about the fragility.

---

[22]https://www.smh.com.au/business/buffett-seeks-major-buys-as-berkshire-profit-gains-20110228-1ba9t.html

Buffett writes, "Leverage, of course, can be lethal to businesses as well. Companies with large debts often assume that these obligations can be refinanced as they mature. That assumption is usually valid. Occasionally, though, either because of company-specific problems or a worldwide shortage of credit, maturities must be met by payment. For that, only cash will do the job. Borrowers then learn that credit is like oxygen. When either is abundant, its presence goes unnoticed. When either is missing, that's all that is noticed. Even a short absence of credit can bring a company to its knees."[23]

EDGE (Technofunda Conviction)

	LOW	HIGH
HIGH	**CORE** Tracking Position	**CORE** Big Bet Average Up Winners
LOW	**NO BET** ✗	**SATELLITE** Tracking Position

ODDS (Reward : Risk)

There are prominent behavioral biases that investors go through and make mistakes related to allocation.

This concept also shows the importance of Risk Management and Exit Strategies which we will learn later in this book.

---

[23]https://www.cbsnews.com/news/5-things-warren-buffett-wants-you-to-do-in-2011/

Allocation mistakes:

- Under-allocation. Due to risk aversion: People prefer to avoid or minimize uncertainty, even at the cost of a lower payoff.

- Over-allocation: Overconfidence bias: People overestimate their knowledge and skills. And Confirmation bias: People search for and interpret information so it confirms one's pre-existing beliefs or hypotheses, while disregarding contrary information and alternative possibilities. Both these biases combined are a potent recipe for over-allocation.

- Overstaying with winners: Endowment effect: this is the tendency to overvalue what you own simply because you own it.

- Overstaying with losers: Loss aversion: People feel twice as bad about losing money as they feel about winning it. This causes investors to hold on to bad choices for far too long, hoping that things will eventually improve and the loss will be avoided.[24]

---

[24]http://institution.motilaloswal.com/emailer/Research/WC21-20161209-MOSL-2011-16-PG044.pdf

CHAPTER SUMMARY

- Successful investors allocate a significant portion of their capital to wins; they put in most of their stakes when they are right.

- All businesses have unforeseen risks; the best risk mitigation strategy is to diversify stocks.

- The minimum stock types in an investor's portfolio range from 15 to 20; this amount of stock provides adequate diversification and meaningful allocation for some gains.

- An average of 19 stocks in a portfolio is the sweet spot; an investor enjoys maximum diversification benefits at this point.

- Investment is a game of probability, and investors think in terms of expected value; every investment avails equal chances for a good or bad outcome.

- A good investor must continue averaging businesses that are performing and trim non-performers.

- Averaging up is complex because of anchoring bias; investors must overcome anchoring bias to succeed.

- Determine the stock allocation size by its price appreciation.

- Correlation between stocks is also essential for diversification—it is a mitigation strategy against geographical risks, currency depreciation, and interest that may hurt a portfolio in one area and benefit it in another.

- The Kelly Criterion is a mathematical formula that gives output on Capital to Bet given win-loss probabilities and payoffs; it is essential in sizing stock in a portfolio.

- The best time to bet big is in an asymmetric payoff—when the probability of winning is high, and the odds are favorable.

- Conversely, avoid betting when the probability of winning and the reward to risk ratio is low.

- An asymmetric payoff is rare; it may be possible in Bear Markets, market anomalies, or on special occasions.

- Subsequent bets are a function of winning the first bet as the overall capital increases.

- Trim out positions when their reward-risk ratio decreases continuously.

- Another variation in Kelly's formula is the edge: the information edge and the analytical edge.

- Blending fundamentals and technicals along with price volume action) provides an information edge.

- Avoid under location due to risk aversion and over-allocation because of overconfidence bias.

YOUR REFLECTIONS

(Reflect on what you have learned and pen down your thoughts)

_____

_____

_____

_____

_____

_____

_____

_____

_____

_____

_____

_____

_____

_____

_____

_____

_____

_____

_____

CHAPTER SIXTEEN
RIDING WINNERS

"To make money in stocks, you need to have the vision to see them, courage to buy them and patience to hold them. Patience is the rarest of the three."
—Thomas Phelps

Each one of us might have bought the likes of Asian Paints, Nestle, Pidilite, Astral Poly, etc., which have created enormous wealth for its shareholders. But why do most of us fail to replicate the same in our portfolio? The simple answer is - we don't ride our winners and do not add capital (averaging up as business keeps performing). This is the biggest mistake most investors make after understanding business selection. Business selection is overrated but holding and adding to great businesses is underrated. Ride your winners, period.

One of the most frequently heard investing advice is to "take some of your winnings off the table", "cash some of the chips" and "book some profits". The idea is that if a stock has gone up significantly, you should sell enough stock to recover your original investment, so you will be left with "free money" which you can afford to lose. Unfortunately, this poor advice has cost many investors a lot of money in opportunity costs, namely mistakes of omission and selling too early.

You can't make big money in stocks if you don't give them a chance to make big money for you. There is nothing easier than making big money in the market once you have latched onto a big winner, because at that point, all you are doing is sitting tight and riding the winners.

It is also wrong to say that one should hold on to a rising stock forever. So let us understand when to sell.

If you apply all the procedures described in this book, a mere handful of Big winners can catapult you to financial independence. Even two or three companies identified with an appropriate allocation in the bull market are sufficient for you to retire.

It is equally important to cut losses quickly. Legendary speculator Jesse Livermore wrote- "You should have a clear target where to sell if the market moves against you. And you must obey your rules! Never sustain a loss of more than 10 percent of your capital.

Losses are twice as expensive to make up. I always established a stop before making a trade."[1]

Our body has several lines of defense- mechanical

---

[1] *Jesse Livermore, How to Trade in Stocks, Greenville: Traders Press, 1991, Page 171*

barriers like skin, chemical barriers like stomach acid and cellular defense like antibodies. Similarly, investors should have multiple lines of defense. Your first line of defense is a stop-loss order, ideally placed when you make the trade, or immediately thereafter. If you fail to limit your risk at inception, make a practice of looking over your positions once every week and selling out at the market (not limit order), all showing a loss. Refinement is not an improvement in the best-case scenario, but an improvement in the worst-case scenario. If your worst-case scenario is not too bad, the gains will take care of themselves. Limiting your downside comes first, and extending your upside comes second.

Bernard Baruch rightly said: "If a speculator is correct half of the time, he is hitting a good average. Even being right 3 or 4 times out of 10 should yield a person a fortune if he has the sense to cut his losses quickly on the ventures where he has been wrong."[2]

George Soros stated aptly- "It's not whether you're right or wrong, but how much money you make when you're right and how much you lose when you're wrong"[3]

William O'Neil suggests a 3:1 ratio of gain:loss, i.e. if your average gain is 20% to 25%, you should cut your losses at 7% or 8%.[4] He continues, "Remember: 7% to 8% is your absolute loss limit. You must sell without hesitation—no waiting a

---

[2]https://marketsmithindia.com/post/secret-to-success-in-the-stock-market

[3]https://www.fincash.com/l/investment/george-soros-quotes-on-successful-investing

[4]William O'Neil, *How to make money in stocks* (New York: McGraw Hill, 2009)

few days to see what might happen; no hoping that the stock will rally back; no need to wait for the day's market close. Nothing but the fact that you're down 7% or 8% below your cost should have a bearing on the situation at this point."[5]

O'Neil further writes, "Institutional investors who lessen their overall risk by taking large positions and diversifying broadly are unable to move into and out of stocks quickly enough to follow such a loss-cutting plan. This is a terrific advantage that you, the nimble and decisive individual investor, have over the institutions. So use it."[6]

Are you getting rich backward? Then you are taking two points of profit and letting your losses run. Why not invert this rule? Limit your risk to one, two or three points and let your profits run.

As they say - Amateurs book profits. Experts book losses.

VALUATION DILEMMA

When investors are invested in great businesses with rapid growth rates, often when the market understands it better, these businesses get re-rated. This might cause optically higher valuation ratios or delusion of overvaluation. As discussed in the chapter on Competitive Advantages, it's sometimes difficult to comprehend these great businesses' long-term mega compounding potential.

---

[5]William O'Neil, *How to make money in stocks* (New York: McGraw Hill, 2009)
[6]William O'Neil, *How to make money in stocks* (New York: McGraw Hill, 2009)

Investors who are too much stuck to the theoretical implication of these valuation ratios often exit too early and these businesses keep creating wealth for a long time. One should not make this mistake. It's better to trail exit and ride them. We will deep dive into this aspect in the Risk Management chapter.

Phil Fisher, in his book *Common Stocks and Uncommon Profits,* explains this aspect:

"How can anyone say with even moderate precision just what is overpriced for an outstanding company with an unusually rapid growth rate? Suppose that instead of selling at twenty-five times earnings, as usually happens, the stock is now at thirty-five times earnings. Perhaps there are new products in the immediate future, the real economic importance of which the financial community has not yet grasped. Perhaps there are not any such products. *If the growth rate is so good that in another ten years the company might well have quadrupled, is it really of such great concern whether at the moment the stock might or might not be 35 percent overpriced? That which really matters is not to disturb a position that is going to be worth a great deal more later.*

...If the job has been correctly done when a common stock is purchased, the time to sell it is—almost never [emphasis added]."[7]

---

[7]Philip A. Fisher, *Common Stocks and Uncommon Profits and Other Writings*, 2nd ed. (Hoboken, NJ: Wiley, 2003)

WHY AVERAGING UP IS IMPORTANT WHILE RIDING WINNERS[8]

From what I have read, economist Vilfredo Federico Damaso Pareto noticed that 20% of the pea plants in his garden generated 80% of the healthy pea pods. Pareto extrapolated this imbalance to other aspects of life and found that roughly 20% of the population controlled 80% of the wealth.

The Pareto Principle is ubiquitous and finds an expression in virtually every aspect of life. Some examples:

20% of the population own 80% of the world's wealth

20% of time spent on various activities produce 80% of the results

20% of customers generally bring in 80% of the revenue

20% of focused employees create 80% of the impact in an organization

Why would this principle, observed in so many spheres of life, not apply to investing? If we observe our investment portfolio, we will witness a similar trend: 20% of stocks in our portfolio generally produce 80% of the returns. To understand this, we need to delve deeper.

Every business begins with an idea before it becomes a start-up. Then comes the journey from a micro-cap to a small-cap to a mid-cap to, eventually, a large-cap.

No matter how brilliant the idea is, or how adaptable and relevant the business is, there are inevitable challenges.

---

[8]https://www.morningstar.in/posts/59579/averaging-important-investing.aspx

Distribution network, supply-chains, deploying the right technology, employee training, management bandwidth, logistics, etc. Not all the companies which started from the idea phase can grow big.

Durgesh Shah shared this during CFA Society Value Investing Summit in 2018:

"There are just 175 Indian companies that make over $100 million (₹ 700 crore) in annual pre-tax profit. Out of these, only 78 companies saw their market value increase 100x. Others may have listed at a decent size or got carved out from a group."[910]

No. of Companies	Owners	100 Baggers	Example
59	Individuals	39	Asian Paints
46	Groups (16)	20	Tata
35	PSU	3	BEL
16	MNC	12	HUL, Nestle
19	Others	4	HDFC Bank

Even if we consider approximately 3,000 decent listed companies, only 5% of companies can scale up extremely well and 20% will scale to a decent extent.

Let's understand the math behind portfolio returns before we figure out how to maximize them.

Portfolio returns are a simple weighted average or sum product of (%) allocation and (%) returns generated. Naturally, we need our winners to have a higher allocation and ride them, at the same time trim laggards to prevent them from dragging portfolio returns.

I quote the legendary Peter Lynch here:

"It's easy to make a mistake and do the opposite, pulling out the flowers and watering the weeds. If you're lucky enough to have one golden egg in your portfolio, it may not matter if you have a couple of rotten ones in with it. Let's say you have a portfolio of six stocks. Two are average, two are below average, and one is a real loser.

But you also have one stellar performer. Your Coca-Cola, your Gillette. A stock that reminds you why you invested.

You need not be right all the time to do well in stocks. If you find one great growth company and own it long enough to let the profits run, the gains should more than offset mediocre results from other stocks in your portfolio."

Retail investors rarely have an information edge. And future predictions are made with great uncertainty. So, it's fair to assume based on the efficient market theory that even if we can select fairly good businesses in our portfolio, at best, we are getting that at a fair price and our predictability of finding stellar performers is like that of tossing a coin (otherwise we would just buy one company and allow it a 100% allocation).

HOW DO WE ENSURE THE HIGHEST ALLOCATION TO WINNERS?

It's only possible by averaging up –adding an allocation to businesses that keep growing and scaling up with time. And this will automatically mean we are not allocating or trimming our laggards in the portfolio. Eventually maximizing portfolio returns. So, we are not only staying invested in our stellar performers - that Coca-Cola, Asian Paints, Pidilite, etc. - but also allocating higher as they become stronger.

As an investor, **how do we manage risk by buying at higher prices?**

It is very important to have an exit strategy in place when averaging up.

Let's say, your initial purchase was at ₹ 100 and had a 30% drawdown threshold for the exit. This means that your initial risk was ₹ 30. If the price moves up to ₹ 200 and you have the same 30% drawdown threshold, your exit price criteria are ₹ 140. So, in either scenario, you take home ₹ 40 as a profit vs. your buying price of ₹ 100. This is known as residual risk and here it is minus 40.

Effectively, if you are averaging up your position at ₹ 200, you are funding it from the negative residual risk of your earlier tranche, and thus your cumulative risk is decreasing as you keep averaging up.

Also, averaging up improves your risk/reward metric. Initially, we take a small position to start with, and if it doesn't work out, we don't give back much. For example, if we take a 1% initial position and it didn't work out as expected and we lost 30%, effectively it's just 0.3% of the capital (1%*30%). But if we win, and keep averaging up, we might have increased the position, sizing to 5% allocation and even 60% of return on full position will increase our capital by 3%.

Hence, the risk/reward is tilted in our favor (1:10 of risk/reward in this example) and the probability of maximizing portfolio returns increases drastically.

Ultimately...

More than stock selection, investing is all about having the probabilities in your favor, having the right mindset and proper execution based on universal mathematical principles. This will give you those 20% winners that will create 80% of returns in your portfolio using the powerful concept of averaging up.[11]

Chatur: In my office, I often see my colleagues, who are keen investors, immersed in the stock indexes for almost the complete day. They are into the habit of buying and selling every day. At times, they are lucky to make a profit, but usually, I hear them hammering their hand on the table. Why are they so impatient that they keep switching lanes?

Aryan: You have got it right, Chatur. They are bitten by the bug called boredom.

---

[11]https://www.morningstar.in/posts/59579/averaging-important-investing.aspx

BOREDOM ARBITRAGE

"People are dying of boredom."

—*Raoul Vaneigem, The Revolution of Everyday Life*

Investors crave activity and stock markets are built on it. And we are surrounded by too much noise due to all sorts of media which makes it seem that we need to act on every piece of information. This is the primary reason investors cannot sit tight and ride their winners.

Investors keep searching for the next big thing and sell their mega compounders. They get bored of the same names of wealth creators. These businesses keep compounding at their own pace, so where is the excitement? And they prematurely sell their compounding machines, which are rare to find. So, how to kill boredom?

We need to practice "Boredom Arbitrage" - having a system or process which lets us ride our winners. I extensively take help from technical indicators like Donchian Channel to objectively suggest when to add to my winners and various other indicators like ATR, PSAR, VStop, EMA, etc., to help me stay in the game until an exit alert is triggered. This way, we can avoid noise, stick to the system and stay focused on the path of mega compounding.

The ecosystem rarely wants you to sit tight, they want you to keep churning so they can charge you fees, brokerage, taxes and sell you stuff. The greatest fortunes come from riding your winners and adding more capital as they keep compounding.

CHAPTER SUMMARY

- Sometimes an investor's portfolio does not reflect the companies they have investments in, although those companies have created enormous wealth for their stakeholders.

- Capitalize on both business selection and averaging up businesses as they keep performing.

- Avoid premature selling and give the stocks time to make big money.

- Know when to sell; do not sit on a rising stock forever.

- Never sustain a loss that is more than 10% of the capital.

- Portfolio refinement is a necessary improvement for a worst-case scenario.

- According to Bernard Baruch, cutting losses quickly on wrong ventures is a wise move.

- William O'Neil states if an investor's average gain is 20% to 25%, they should cut their losses when the profits drop to 7% or 8%.

- O'Neil also states having large positions and broad diversification slows down the loss-cutting plan.

- There is a valuation dilemma for re-rated businesses with investors and rapid growth rates; such conditions lead to overvaluation.

- Investors usually exit too early from such investments because of over-reliance on the theoretical implications of these valuations instead of having a better exit trail and riding winners for long.

- Averaging up is crucial while riding winners because businesses take time to grow a larger market cap from inception, regardless of the nature of the business idea.

- Portfolio returns are the weighted average or sum product of percentage allocation and percentage returns generated.

- Winners in a portfolio need a higher allocation for the investor to ride, and laggards require trimming to keep them from dragging the portfolio.

- The only way winners can get a higher allocation in a portfolio is by averaging up.

- Additionally, have an exit strategy while averaging up.

- Averaging up reduces negative residual risks and improves the investor's risk to reward metric.

- Aside from stock selection, investing is about having a favorable probability.

- Investors can resist premature selling and ride their winners by practicing Boredom Arbitrage.

- Technical indicators are excellent Boredom Arbitrage tools; by focusing on ATR, PSAR, VStop, or EMA, an investor can stay put until exit triggers become loud.

YOUR REFLECTIONS

(Reflect on what you have learned and pen down your
thoughts)

_____

_____

_____

_____

_____

_____

_____

_____

_____

_____

_____

_____

_____

_____

_____

_____

_____

_____

_____

_____

CHAPTER SEVENTEEN

RISK MANAGEMENT, REBALANCING AND EXIT STRATEGIES

"Rome was not built in a day but Hiroshima and Nagasaki were destroyed in a day."
—*Vijay Kedia*[1]

It takes years to build a great portfolio and create wealth, but if there is no Risk Management in place, it can destroy our wealth in seconds. Risk management is of paramount importance in the investing journey. We all, as investors, are risk managers. Our key job is to protect the downside, and the upside will take care of itself.

---

[1]https://economictimes.indiatimes.com/wealth/invest/why-you-should-not-invest-in-junk-stocks/articleshow/57452293.cms

As Howard Marks has rightly mentioned in his book *The Most Important Thing*[2]

"Investing consists of exactly one thing: dealing with the future. And because none of us can know the future with certainty, the risk is inescapable. Thus, dealing with risk is an essential-I think *the* essential - element in investing. It's easy to find investments that might go up. If you can find enough of these, you'll have moved in the right direction. But you are unlikely to succeed for long if you haven't dealt explicitly with risk. The first step consists of understanding it. The second step is recognizing when it's high. The critical final step is controlling it."

Now, you might wonder what is meant by risk. Howard Marks explains, "In the investment world, we talk about risk all the time, but there's no universal agreement about what risk is or what it should imply for investors' behavior. Some people think the risk is the likelihood of losing money, and others (including many finance academics) think the risk is the volatility of asset prices or returns. And there are many other kinds of risk—too many to cover here. I lean heavily toward the first definition: in my view, the risk is primarily the likelihood of permanent capital loss. But there's also such a thing as opportunity risk: the likelihood of missing out on potential gains. Put the two together and we see that risk is the possibility of things not going the way we want."[3]

Thus, the risk is the possibility of events turning out, so it is different from what we expect.

---

[2]Howard Marks, *The Most Important Thing* (New York: Columbia University Press, 2011)

[3]Howard Marks, *Mastering The Market Cycle* (HarperCollins, 2018)

Now, think about what do we control as an investor? We have no control over returns, no control over the business performance or macro events. However, the three key things we can control are:

1. Allocation - how much to allocate and sizing our position

2. Downside Risk - how much amount to lose on each investment

3. Our Behavior - how we react to different external situations

UNDERSTANDING RISK IN HIGH GROWTH QUALITY BUSINESSES

Warren Buffett said at the University of Florida in 1998: "Coke Cola IPO-ed in 1919 for $40. A year later, it was $19. You can always find a few reasons why that was not a good time to buy it, but if you bought 1 share at $40 and reinvested the dividends, you would have $5 million today. This factor overrides everything macro concerns you could have. There is never a perfect time to buy a great business; there is always a reason to worry, but you should also know when it is wise to worry at all. For things that are unimportant or unknown, you should not worry. If you are right about the business, you will make a lot of money over time."[4]

For 17 years after his speech, the stock price return of Coca Cola was 23%. Impressive, right? But consider this: the stock of Coca Cola did not return 23% CAGR, but an absolute 23% for the entire period! This shows that even

---

[4]https://www.tilsonfunds.com/BuffettUofFloridaspeech.pdf

high-quality Banyan tree businesses have their risks of periodic underperformance.

Although we focus on high-quality businesses in the core portfolio, we need to understand that businesses change, disruption is for real and even faster. As an investor, the general goal is to identify companies with excellent earnings growth at reasonable prices and expectations this will last for the long term.

Now, let's take an example of 2003-2008 wealth creators. Some of the quality and highly respected names were Reliance Industries, BHEL, Bharti Airtel, L&T, Unitech, Essar Oil, Hindustan Unilever, Neyveli Lignite, Tata Communications, MRPL, Aban Offshore, Zee Entertainment, Essar Shipping, Sterlite Industries, HDFC Bank, Wipro, Infosys, etc.

PAT CAGR of most of the above names in 2003-2008 was more than 25-30%. These were India's great companies with a great outlook for even future growth. They were also richly valued as investors thought the party would go on.

Fast-forward now, after more than a decade, where are most of these companies? What went wrong? For most of them, growth faltered. Names like Bharti Airtel, Tata Communications, Aban Offshore, etc., got decimated by disruption in the sector. Others like Reliance Industries, Hindustan Unilever, Wipro, etc., had to struggle for growth. Some even went on the verge of bankruptcy.

This reminds me of that quote from Bill Gates:

"WE ALWAYS OVERESTIMATE THE CHANGE THAT WILL OCCUR IN THE NEXT TWO YEARS AND UNDERESTIMATE THE CHANGE THAT WILL OCCUR

IN THE NEXT TEN. DON'T LET YOURSELF BE LULLED INTO INACTION."

The idea is to be constantly vigil - act when needed. Have risk management and exit strategy in place even if we have bought great quality growth businesses in our portfolio.

Here are examples of what happens when growth goes away and why we need to be vigilant.

EXAMPLE 1: BHARTI AIRTEL - THE LOST DECADE

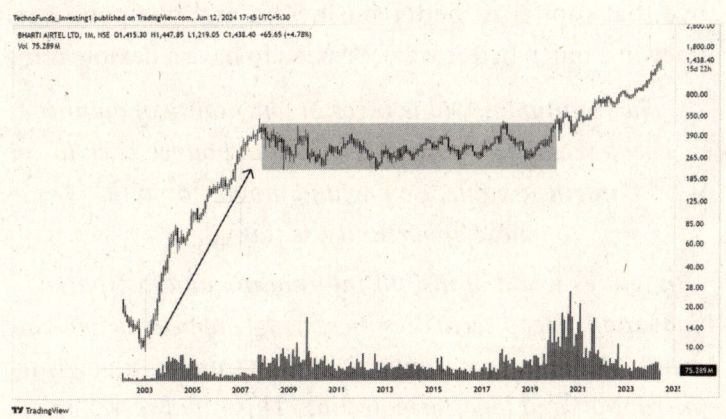

EXAMPLE -2: ABBAN OFFSHORE - THE DEAD SOULS

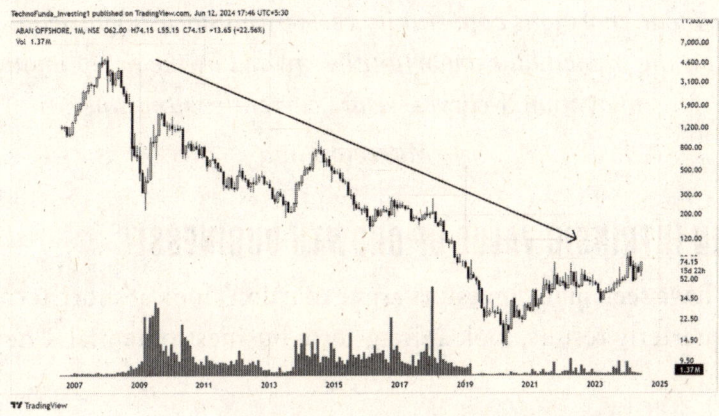

NO ROOM FOR HOPE STORIES

Often, we have price anchoring in our minds. As humans, we are always hopeful and hope has helped us evolve and survive in the toughest of times. But in investing, it's dangerous most of the time. If we just hope these past winners will somehow come back and survive, we are mistaken. If data says that business is deteriorating and we made a mistake, we need to get out. Follow risk management. And yes, one can always re-enter if the business performs again. Alternatively, we can move that capital to better businesses and compound our money in a much better way. We need to have a flexible mind.

"The traditional "value investor" mentality of buying cheap securities, waiting for them to bounce back to "intrinsic value," selling and moving onto the next opportunity, is flawed.

In today's world of instant information and fast-paced innovation, cheap securities increasingly appear to be value traps; often they are companies ailing from technological disruption and long-term decline. This rapid recycling of capital also creates an enormous drag on our after-tax returns. In addition, by focusing on these opportunities, we incur enormous opportunity costs by not focusing instead on the tremendous opportunities created by the exceptional innovation S-curves we are currently witnessing."

—Marcelo Lima

ON INTRINSIC VALUE OF GROWTH BUSINESSES

I have seen many investors argue that don't look at short-term quarterly results, look at long-term business potential. They have also done the homework to find the intrinsic value of a business by applying methods like DCF (Discounted Cash Flows, etc.), which has so many underlying assumptions on growth, interest rates, terminal value, etc.

Literally, value changes every day as information and variables affecting businesses keep changing. One cannot anchor to old data of intrinsic value to make future decisions.

As Howard Marks has rightly mentioned in his book *The Most Important Thing*[5]

"In Investing, as in life, there are very few sure things. Values can evaporate, estimates can be wrong, circumstances can change and "sure things" can fail. However, there are two concepts we can hold to with confidence:

Rule number one: Most things will prove cyclical.

Rule number two: some of the greatest opportunities for gain and loss come when other people forget rule number one."

REBALANCING

During a market crash, one should rebalance the portfolio to increase allocation to companies that have undergone high drawdowns (we can finance this investment by reducing allocations to companies that have not undergone high drawdowns).

---

[5]Howard Marks, *The Most Important Thing* (New York: Columbia University Press, 2011)

EXIT CRITERIA

My simple logic is, if we want to take buying decisions on such businesses, we need to continuously re-evaluate the intrinsic value which most investors don't do. They are fixated on old calculations and do not incorporate reality.

We need to learn from a 260-year-old mathematical equation called Baye's Rule. Also known as conditional probability, it measures the probability of an event, given that another event has occurred.

Below is the simplified version which Daniel Kahneman shared in his book *Thinking fast and slow:*

Posterior odds = Prior odds × Likelihood ratio

where, the posterior odds = the odds (the ratio of probabilities) for two competing hypotheses.

Prior Odds are Base Rates (i.e. historical statistical information)

The likelihood ratio is information specific to the current situation being examined

So, there are 2 parts to it:

1. If there are strong low base rates (for example, the odds of an airline company creating wealth for shareholders is too low), will you invest in an airline business where there is a powerful positive narrative around the business or situation you are examining?

2. If there are strong high base rates (for example, the odds of a consumer durables company creating wealth is too high), and there is new strong evidence

of corporate governance around the situation you are examining, will you sell or avoid it?

Basically, what Baye's rule tells you is that we need to follow a balanced approach.

As Charlie Munger rightly said when he was asked about the process to read annual reports:

"You have to have some idea of why you're looking for the information. Don't read annual reports the way Francis Bacon said you do science—which, by the way, is not the way that you do science—where you just collect endless (amounts of) data and then only later do you try to make sense of it. You have to start with some ideas about reality. And then you have to look to see whether what you're seeing fits in with that basic thought structure. Frequently, you'll look at a business having fabulous results. And the question is, "How long can this continue?" Well, there's only one way I know of to do that. And that's to think about why the results are occurring now – and then to figure out the forces that could cause those results to stop occurring."[6]

Also, as we understood from a discussion on growth and disruption, it's impossible to predict growth after 5-10-15 years. And disruption can make the terminal value go to zero overnight, which forms a major part of intrinsic value.

Bottom line: We need to have an objective exit strategy for such businesses. I use a combination of technical indicators to alert me and then go back to fundamentals to understand

---

[6]Charlie Munger at *39th Annual meeting of Wesco Financial Shareholders in 1998*

business deterioration. Capital protection is the most underrated concept in investing community.

Example:

I have used a simple indicator called EMA (Exponential Moving Average) on a monthly time frame to help us take exit decisions on Zee Entertainment. See how it helped us in riding the growth phase and then exit with little capital erosion.

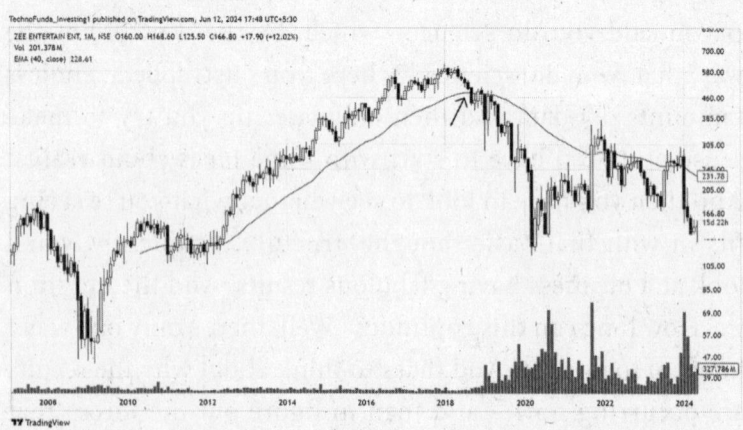

We can use multiple such indicators like ATR, PSAR, VStop, EMA, etc., to take exit decisions. Again, we can use different timeframes based on our tree classification (remember - Banyan, Mango, Bamboo, Cactus, Weeds and Palm) to sync it with the fundamental business model of the company.

Over the years, I have understood that we need to have a framework for the selling process, just like how we have for buying the shares. Based on our tree classification, here is my broad thought process (and this keeps evolving) on how to make a sell decision:

WHEN TO SELL CACTUS BUSINESS CATEGORY

These are typically low growth and low RoCE companies. I rarely prefer to buy them in the first place, as the more you hold them, the more it harms your portfolio returns.

If I have bought any businesses which might have been either Mango or Banyan with high growth and it starts turning to Cactus, I would watch for the fundamental signs given below along with technical indicators mentioned earlier to sell:

- The company getting affected by competition and losing pricing power as well as growth
- Lack of new products and company getting affected by disruption in the industry
- Loss of market share for a prolonged period of time
- Bad capital allocation decisions like unrelated acquisitions, reinvesting cash flows in low RoCE businesses, etc.

WHEN TO SELL MANGO BUSINESS CATEGORY

This category is generally a very small percentage of the portfolio. The purpose is mainly capital protection and sometimes defensive play during bear markets or periods of high macroeconomic uncertainty.

As they are generally stable businesses with predictable cash flows, the fluctuation in the share prices is generally a function of overall P/E multiple swings that occur due to different market conditions. Then, it again reverts to meaning.

The selling decision here can be considered by the below factors:

- When it goes into high P/E territory due to extreme euphoria in the overall sector or broader market condition but business growth is the same; we can trail our exits in such scenarios to make most of the euphoria

- Sometimes the return ratios deteriorate due to the erosion of competitive advantages and it's time to consider selling

- Overall portfolio allocation decision is changed from capital protection to high growth focus when you get Banyan businesses at lesser valuation like market corrections or bear market

- When similar businesses are available at attractive valuations

- Instead of giving back free cash flow as dividends/buyback, if management starts misallocating capital, it's time to sell

WHEN TO SELL BANYAN BUSINESS CATEGORY

Ideally, we should be holding these businesses as it keeps compounding and performing. But we know that the world is dynamic. Disruptions are even faster and things can go wrong.

Below are key parameters to consider while taking Banyan Business selling decision:

- Structural impairment to future growth due to various reasons like disruption, saturation in the market, lack of innovation, etc., (basically Banyan turning into the Mango category)

- Management change: top-performing management exiting the company

- Erosion of competitive advantages

- Profitable reinvestment opportunities are missing, and the company starts returning significant capital to shareholders or starts misallocating capital

WHEN TO SELL BAMBOO BUSINESS CATEGORY

As we discussed earlier, the Bamboo category is majorly to experiment and test businesses under potential transition to better categories like Mango or Banyan. Sell decisions are more frequent here as we need to understand these are satellite plays with a low probability of structural shift.

Another key point to consider is that although the structural transition to Banyan may fail, if the business shows significant improvement from Cactus or Weeds, it can get re-rated fast and once it disappoints, then it can get de-rated very quickly. Idea is to stay agile and vigilant with the exit process here.

Some of the key parameters to focus on selling decisions for this category:

- Initial improvement is business fades away due to competition or sector headwinds

- Sector Tailwind was a major driver of improvement and, if that reverts to mean

- Company struggling to find reinvestment opportunities beyond the initial stage

- Execution of earnings triggers is not done properly to translate into structural growth

- When improvement in earnings growth and RoCE proves to be temporary in nature

WHEN TO SELL PALM BUSINESS CATEGORY

These are typical cyclical stocks. Entry and exits are extremely critical here and one should take a position in these types of businesses after carefully learning the traits of these businesses. Technical exit indicators on daily charts are generally best used for this category to make faster decisions.

Some of the key points for selling decision for this category are:

- When these cyclical businesses are termed as structural long-term growth stories

- When PE multiple looks optically very low compared to peak earnings

- The demand starts to collapse or the supply picks up or both. Remember, it's mainly a play on the demand-supply equilibrium

- Existing plants in the sector are running at full capacity and new capacities are coming into operation

- Margins peaks and end-user industries shut down due to high input costs

WHEN TO SELL WEEDS BUSINESS CATEGORY

In the first place, we should not be owning these businesses. Even if the business has become weed-like by transitioning from Mango or Banyan, it should have been sold much earlier when signs are visible. The best time to exit weed stocks was yesterday; the second-best time is today. Exit them! Not tomorrow. Not today. Now. It's like asking for how much time we should hold stinking garbage in our house - throw it out NOW.

CHAPTER SUMMARY

- Wealth takes years to build, but it can perish in seconds without risk management.

- There are three steps to dealing with risk management: understand, recognize, and control risks.

- Risk is the possibility that things may not go as planned, expected, or desired.

- While investors have zero control over returns, business performance, or macro events, they control allocation, downsizing risks, and their behavior.

- It is crucial to remain vigilant as an investor; develop risk management and exit strategy regardless of the quality growth of businesses in the portfolio.

- Adhere to risk management, not hope; when data says it is time to exist, do not linger around.

- Remember re-entering is always an option.

- The intrinsic value of business growth is dynamic because variables keep changing; therefore, you cannot use old data for future decisions.

- Two important investment principles are that most processes are cyclical, and wins and losses occur when investors forget the first principle.

- In case of a market crash, increase allocation to companies with higher high drawdowns.

- Have an objective exit strategy.

- Sell the cactus business stock when it loses pricing power because of the competition, lack new products, experience industry disruptions, get prolonged market share loss, and evidence of poor capital allocation.

- Sell mango business category when it goes into high P/E territory, return ratios decrease because of erosion from the competition, allocation decision changes from capital protection to high growth focus, similar businesses are available at attractive valuations, and when management misallocates funds

- Sell Bunyan when there is structural impairment to future growth, management change, decrease in competitive advantages, and profitable investment opportunities.

- Sell bamboo when the competition and other headwinds impair initial business improvement. When sector tailwinds revert to mean unavailable reinvestment opportunities, execution of earnings triggers does not translate to structural growth. Earnings growth and ROCE improvement are temporary.

- Sell palm when cyclical businesses become structural long-term growth stories, P/E translates to low peak earnings, demand dwindles or supply increases, there is an easy market entry, margins peak, and the end-user industry shuts down.

YOUR REFLECTIONS

(Reflect on what you have learned and pen down your thoughts)

_____

_____

_____

_____

_____

_____

_____

_____

_____

_____

_____

_____

_____

_____

_____

_____

_____

CHAPTER EIGHTEEN

VICARIOUS LEARNING - LEARN FROM OTHER'S MISTAKES

*"You don't have to pee on an electric fence
to learn not to do it."*

—Charlie Munger

We generally overestimate the power of learning and doing things ourselves, but underestimate the power of observation, learning from others' mistakes - Vicarious Learning. Particularly, it is very important with markets and investing, where mistakes are very costly and result in monetary loss.

Morgan Housel writes:

"Everything's been done before. The scenes change but the behaviors and outcomes don't. Historian Niall Ferguson's plug for his profession is that "The dead outnumber the living 14 to 1, and we ignore the accumulated experience of such a huge majority of mankind at our peril." The biggest lesson from the 100 billion people who are no longer alive is that they tried everything we're trying. The details were different, but they tried to outwit entrenched competition. They swung from optimism to pessimism at the worst times. They battled unsuccessfully against the reversion of mean. They learned that popular things seem safe because so many people are involved, but they're most dangerous because they're most competitive. The same stuff that guides today and will guide tomorrow. History is abused when specific events are a guide to the future. It's way more useful as a benchmark for how people react to risk and incentives, which is stable over time."[1]

I have listed down 10 powerful mistakes which we can learn from. These are again my vicarious learning and some I have made myself.

The acronym to remember these mistakes is - CHALLENGES

1. C - Cheap Trap

2. H - Holding Hope Stories; Loss Aversion

3. A - Averaging Down Losers

---

[1]Morgan Housel, *"Ideas That Changed My Life"*, Collaborative Fund (blog), March 7, 2018, https://www.collaborativefund.com/blog/ideas-that-changed-my-life/

4. L - Lack of Process or System

5. L - Leverage; Overconfidence

6. E - Extrapolating Past

7. N - Next HDFC Syndrome

8. G - Gambling; Lure of Quick Money; Tips

9. E - Emotional Attachment

10. S - Selling Winners too Early

1. CHEAP TRAP

Many investors get fixated on past prices and when a stock is declining (particularly much more than the market fall), the perception is that the stock has become cheaper. Optically, even the PE ratio based on past earnings looks low. This is generally a trap. My friend bought shares of Indiabulls Housing Finance in late 2018 when the stock was making 52-week lows after awesome ~6x returns during 2014-17. The low made in 2018 was ₹ 640 (compared to 2017 all-time high of ₹ 1400. He thought he bought it cheap, but it never came back to that price. Earnings deteriorated in the next 3 years and in February 2022, it was trading ₹ 150.

Understand that proven quality companies are seldom available too cheap, particularly when the broader market is not falling much.

Many investors even have the notion of buying low-priced stocks, thinking they are buying cheap. They will always be on the lookout for companies trading less than ₹ 10-20 (also popularly known as penny stocks) and they hesitate to buy the shares of companies that are priced high, e.g., MRF,

Eicher Motors, Page Industries, etc. They ignore the concept of market cap or valuation multiple and always think that cheap price means cheap valuation. This is far, far away from the truth and should be avoided.

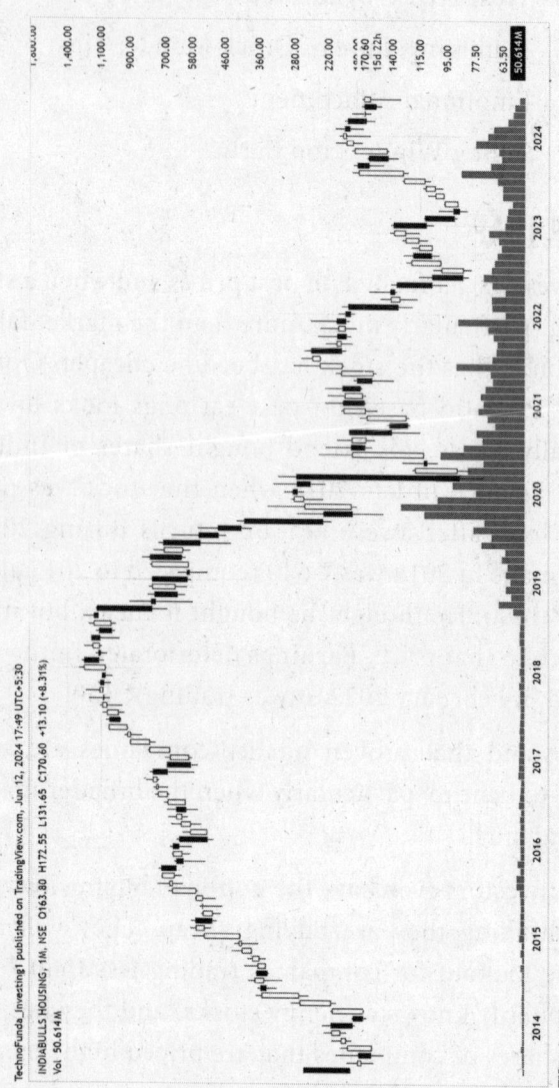

The most common logic given for buying low-priced stocks is - how much more it can fall? - I call it *"Aur Kitna Niche Jayega"* syndrome. Well, technically, it can go down another 100% from the buying price..!! Think about it.

2. HOLDING HOPE STORIES; LOSS AVERSION

In today's time, we are blessed with the speed at which we get information. We might have bought a company during its good times and then slowly things change, businesses saturate or deteriorate. The best part is we see the results not promising and now slowly we are turning into losses.

Logically, we should be selling the position and finding a better-performing company, but then our mind plays the game. We become averse to booking the loss and keep holding hoping someday something will happen even if no growth triggers are visible.

In such scenarios, we not only forgo the opportunity cost of our capital, but sometimes it results in a huge loss if business deterioration continues, which usually does happen.

> *"If you take the best text in economics by Mankiw, he says intelligent people make decisions based on opportunity costs—in other words, it's your alternatives that matter. That's how we make all of our decisions."*
>
> **—Charlie Munger**

Remember, capital is finite and we are in the business of finding the best possible opportunity for that capital corresponding to the risk we are taking. Sticking to hope stories is extremely injurious to your portfolio returns, and thereby, your long-term wealth creation goals.

Example: Bharti Airtel had excellent business growth with PAT CAGR of >30% during its good times in 2003-2008 (with ~45x returns from 2003 low until it's high in 2007). Then the sector became extremely competitive, starting with the entry of Tata Docomo with its disruptive pricing, followed by the entry of Jio, issues around spectrum allotment and many internal execution challenges. For the next decade, the hope investors would have hardly made any money.

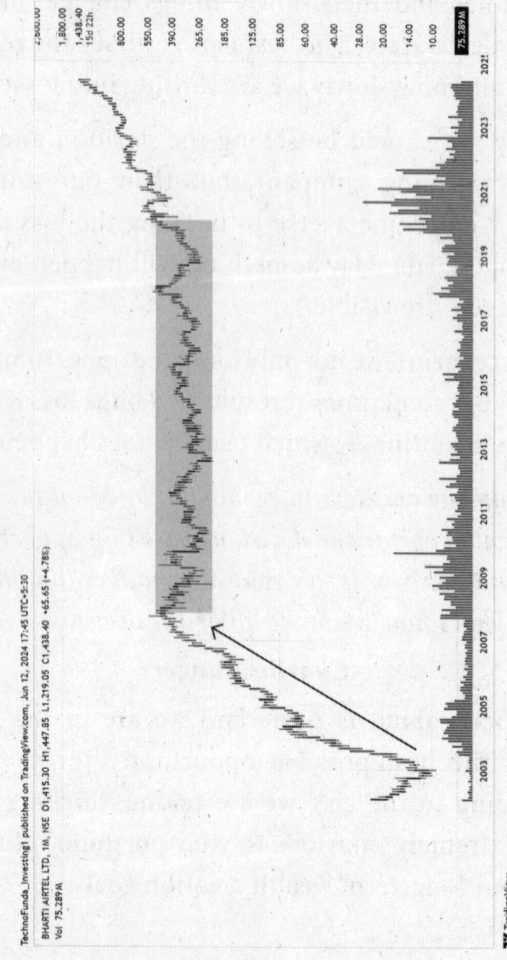

As Dan Sullivan has rightly said:

"The difference between successful investors and unsuccessful investors is how they react to being invested in a losing stock. There is absolutely no reason to allow a mistake to become an ego-shattering experience. Being wrong is not a problem. Making mistakes is not the problem. The problem is being unwilling to accept the mistake. The problem is staying wrong."

Being wrong is not a mistake. *Staying* wrong is.

3. AVERAGING DOWN LOSERS

This is one of the worst mistakes investors make, and it can cause a permanent loss of capital. Let's say, investors are buying shares at ₹ 100 and then again when it falls further to ₹ 50 due to business deterioration or potential future growth issues. They think that they are averaging out the cost and bringing it down to ₹ 75 but in reality; they are chasing losers with their good capital. As they say - throwing good money after bad.

Think about the eventual outcome: if you keep doing this, say at ₹ 25, then ₹ 10 and then ₹ 2, what will happen? The majority of the portfolio will have capital allocated to losers and winners will suffer as they don't get incremental capital. This is surely a recipe for disaster.

Let's take the example of Aban Offshore. It had a great run in the bull market of 2003-2008. In its good times, from say 2006-2007, it became ~10x and earnings were very strong thanks to underlying oil and gas industry tailwinds.

Later, the company struggled for growth and made huge losses from 2015-16. From its peak of 2007 which was ₹ 5500, it came crumbling down to ₹ 13 during the Mar-2020 fall. Imagine what would happen if someone kept averaging down this stock for the last 10-12 years?

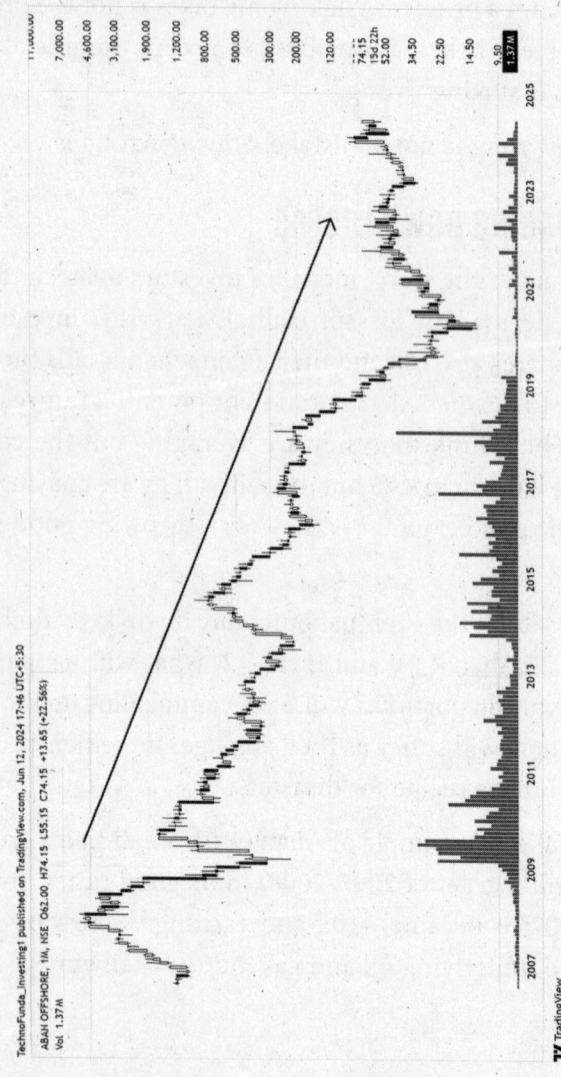

I believe we should keep averaging up instead of averaging down. As business improves, we should not anchor ourselves to historical prices, but if the business has become better than earlier, we should put capital to work behind them.

Peter Lynch has rightly mentioned in his book *One Up on Wall Street*:

"Consistent winners raise their bet as their position strengthens, and they exit the game when the odds are against them, while consistent losers hand on until the bitter end of every expensive pot, hoping for miracles and enjoying the thrill of defeat. In stud poker and on Wall Street, miracles happen just often enough to keep the losers losing."

According to Mark Minervini, "Remember that only losers average losers."[2]

4. LACK OF PROCESS OR SYSTEM

Now, this is one of the most important parts of investing, i.e., having a system in place. It means, we should have a proper framework around stock screening, buying decisions, when to add and exit decisions. In earlier chapters, I have shared the broad process of portfolio allocation, i.e. core-satellite along with the screening process (remember MACHINE) and we also covered various portfolio allocation as well as position sizing principles. Finally, we also thumbed through the importance of risk management. Having clarity in the end-to-end process helps us remain decluttered from noise,

---

[2] Mark Minervini, *Trade like a stock market wizard* (New York: McGraw Hill, 2013)

follow our rules during panic situations and always remain objective.

However, it is important to note that just building a system or having a process is not important, but having the discipline to follow and keep refining the same is very critical. Also, this system should be in sync with one's personality.

> *"Complexity is about tactics; simplicity is about systems. Tactics come and go but an overarching philosophy about the way the world works can help you make better decisions in multiple scenarios. Simple doesn't go out of style but complex does."*
>
> —*Ben Carlson*

Another advantage of building systems or processes is that it will help you avoid noise. There is so much overwhelming information around us, particularly during uncertain times and with a lack of a system, it will overpower us.

Nassim Nicholas Taleb writes, in his book Fooled by Randomness, "Minimal exposure to media should be the guiding principle for someone involved in decision making under uncertainty - including all participants in financial markets."[3]

5. LEVERAGE; OVERCONFIDENCE

Many investors become overconfident when everything is going fine. They feel they know it all. And even worse, they take leverage in the lure of making quick money. They ignore or underestimate risk.

---

[3]Nassim Nicholas Taleb, *Fooled by Randomness: The Hidden Role of Chance in Life and in the Markets* (New York: Random House, 2005)

Morgan Housel has rightly pointed out:

"Your personal experiences make up maybe 0.00000001% of what's happened in the world but maybe 80% of how you think the world works. People believe what they've seen it happen exponentially more than what they read about has happened to other people if they read about other people at all. We're all biased to our own personal history. Everyone. If you've lived through hyperinflation, or a 50% bear market, or were born to rich parents, or have been discriminated against, you both understand something that people who haven't experienced those things never will, but you'll also likely overestimate the prevalence of those things happening again or happening to other people."[4]

6. EXTRAPOLATING PAST

This is again a very common mistake investors make. We get too fixated on past winners, past performance and try to extrapolate that in the future to justify our buying decision. This thought process can lead to disaster, particularly in the following scenarios:

(a) When high growth, high-quality Banyan is transitioning to Mango (low growth), it could be due to industry headwinds, disruption in business model, competitive intensity or simply due to lack of execution. Sometimes, they will have deceptive relatively low PE just before the earnings collapse.

---

[4]Morgan Housel, *"Ideas That Changed My Life"*, Collaborative Fund (blog), March 7, 2018, https://www.collaborativefund.com/blog/ideas-that-changed-my-life/

(b) Cyclical sectors when a stock is around the peak of its earnings and everything looks perfect. And investors think of this as structural growth that will continue for years.

In both these scenarios, there could be a sharp fall in earnings growth coupled with PE de-rating (remember - for cyclicals, you need to see PE based on mean earnings over a cycle and not using peak earnings).

> *"Just as styles in women's gowns and hats and costume jewelry are forever changing with time, the old leaders of the stock market are dropped and new ones rise to take their places...In the course of time new leaders will come to the front: some of the old leaders will be dropped. It will always be that way if there is a stock market...Keep mentally flexible. Remember the leaders of today may not be the leaders two years from now."*
>
> —*Jesse Livermore*

7. NEXT HDFC SYNDROME

We have discussed in earlier chapters about the Banyan type businesses, i.e., great businesses with Reinvestment Moats, which can keep reinvesting capital at high rates. These are a minority. And the best part is they keep compounding for a long time in the future.

But again, investors are bored of listening to the same compounding names and they feel they can find another HDFC mega compounder and get lured by stories that vested parties keep pumping. And the result is obvious, great businesses are not just made from stories, it takes a confluence of many factors to become great businesses. It is difficult.

Example: Many investors kept chasing Yes Bank and DHFL, thinking of them as the next HDFC Bank and the next GRUH finance (this has got merged with Bandhan Bank). We all know the outcome.

You need not sell your gems just because they have doubled or tripled so soon in the quest for the next HDFC where the caliber is not yet proven. You just need to keep riding it until the business deteriorates - 'next HDFC is probably again HDFC'.

8. GAMBLING; LURE OF QUICK MONEY; TIPS

This is one of the biggest mistakes that not only starters but even experts make - getting carried away in the lure of Quick Money. I would admit that I have made most of these mistakes during my investing journey, which I am sharing here.

   a. The most prominent one during bull markets is chasing shares of "hot" IPO for quick money, i.e., listing gains. We have seen that euphoria in 2008 when Reliance Power came with IPO and it again repeats. We saw in 2022 when again investors rushed for overvalued technology platform IPOs. This is generally coupled with the "hot" sector, where there is a mad rush from the investing community.

   b. Gambling or speculating on the direction of shares - whether it will go up or down in the next few seconds, minutes or hours is again suicidal. It's a zero-sum game. Add to it the underlying leveraged instruments like F&O, high margin products can create a permanent loss of capital in a very short period.

c. Buying shares of random companies on tips and multi-bagger recommendations for quick money doing no research is another area where most investors get trapped. They lose their hard-earned money.

I have seen that many investors are averse to learning, they are tight-fisted about investing in their own education around investing. The result: they pay much higher tuition fees to market by incurring huge losses.

9. EMOTIONAL ATTACHMENT

One should never mix emotions with financial decisions. The biggest financial mistakes are made when emotions become part of the Decision Process. You should not have an emotional attachment to a company's shares, for example, because they were gifted to you by your parents. The stock doesn't know you own it. Similarly, one should not get carried away with an attachment towards the company's promoters. As Gautam Baid writes- "I wish I had read Cialdini's book before I made my investment in Virat Crane Industries in 2016. I felt emotionally attached to its founder, Grandhi Subba Rao, after I read about his life story of hardship, struggle, and perseverance. My strong liking bias for the promoter in turn drove confirmation bias, and I began to justify my entry into the stock by considering only the positive points and completely sidelining various negative aspects, such as low margins and related-party transactions, even though I was aware of them."[5]

10. SELLING WINNERS TOO EARLY

If you watch the interviews of several successful investors, this is the biggest mistake they all regret. One always underestimates how high a stock can go. A stock that goes up 100 times first doubles and then goes up another 50 times! There is Temptation to book profits, but wise investors know that doing this is the exact opposite of rational behavior. Following the trailing stop loss method enables you to make the most out of the winner. Perhaps the biggest regret investors have is not holding a winner for long enough. Finding a hundred baggers is about the vision to see, the courage to buy, and the patience to hold; the third is probably the most difficult yet the most important.

---

[5]Gautam Baid, *The Joys of Compounding* (New York, Columbia University Press, 2020)

CHAPTER SUMMARY

- Vicarious learning happens through observation and drawing lessons from the mistakes of others; it is crucial in marketing and investment because mistakes are costly.

- A cheap trap is a fixation on past stock earnings when prices are declining; even the P/E ratio based on past earnings is always low.

- Investors forgo their capital opportunity cost and expose themselves to huge losses when holding hope on stocks despite data showing to implement an exit strategy.

- Averaging down losers is the worst mistake an investor can make; it takes away capital allocated to winners, denying them the opportunity for incremental capital while compounding losses.

- The lack of a process or system for stock screening, buying, adding and exiting decisions, and so forth, brings confusion in strategy and execution.

- It is wise not to become overconfident or take leverage to make quick money when everything is running smoothly.

- Avoid extrapolating the past; when investors fixate on past winners and performance, they project the outdated data to the future to justify their buying strategy, and the outcome is always disastrous.

- Great businesses and investment moves are not a by-product of stories—sometimes investors get lured into the next HDFC syndrome because of boredom from the monotony of investing with the same players and rules.

- The allure of quick money can send investors into a gambling frenzy; common gambling incentives include chasing hot IPO shares in bull markets—it never ends well.

- Never mix emotions with financial decisions because mistakes are rampant when feelings get intertwined.

- It is wise not to attach sentimental value to investment, even when shares have sentimental value because they were a gift; similarly, do not get attached to a promoter.

- Never underestimate how high a stock can rise; it leads to the quick selling of winners.

- Investors always regret giving up their shares too quickly because of underestimation.

YOUR REFLECTIONS

(Reflect on what you have learned and pen down your thoughts)

_____

_____

_____

_____

_____

_____

_____

_____

_____

_____

_____

_____

_____

_____

_____

_____

_____

CHAPTER NINETEEN

THE MOST IMPORTANT THING

"I fear not the man who has practiced 10,000 kicks once, but I fear the man who has practiced one kick 10,000 times."
—Bruce Lee

Investing is simple, but not easy! Why is it so?

When I started my journey, I started with intraday and F&O. On some days, I made a lot of money. On others, it was terrible to the extent that on a few instances, my entire monthly salary got exhausted in just 1-2 days.

I was getting frustrated, I could not eat my food or sleep properly, I used to get angry without reason...yes...I have been through that. I even blew off my entire capital. The stress and pain were too much.

Then I tried my hands on investing, again the same thing. I fell flat on my face. And I was about to quit, but thought, I will try it.

I quit my job with no savings. Thereafter, I surrendered myself to my mentors and went through the grind. Read many books. Tested many things. Changed my mindset. Changed my belief systems.

And...

Things started to change. I got the path. I worked on my mindset. Created systems.

I always thought it was the outside world stopping me. But I was wrong, it was ME. It was my mindset, my belief systems, my thoughts that were barricading me from getting great results. And then there was no looking back.

As an investor, we always look for the holy grail, the next big multi-bagger, the next best strategy, the next best system. We have also seen many investors disputing which investing style is the best, whether it is value investing, growth investing, momentum investing, technofunda investing or any other similar streams.

The truth is, it is never about investing philosophy, it's about how well one executes it, how well one understands it, how well it is in sync with one's mindset. And this requires dedication, a winning mindset and most importantly - implementation by practicing it.

In his book *Outliers*, Malcolm Gladwell mentioned that the difference between those who succeed and those who do not is 10,000 hours. One needs to put at least 10,000 hours (which is roughly 5 years) to master the craft. There are no shortcuts in life. Yes, some can do faster or slower, but mastering your investing style is very important. Many investors ignore this aspect and then blame the system.

I am sure you will implement what I have shared with you and practice it to achieve excellence in your investing journey.

Believe in yourself. Be Prepared. Implement your learnings. Trust your process. Achieve excellence.

"More important than the will to win is the will to prepare."

—*Charlie Munger*

Let me conclude this chapter with a powerful insight shared by Friedrich Nietzsche:

"Because we think well of ourselves, but nonetheless never suppose ourselves capable of producing a painting like one of Raphael's or a dramatic scene like one of Shakespeare's, we convince ourselves that the capacity to do so is quite extraordinarily marvelous, a wholly uncommon accident, or, if we are still religiously inclined, a mercy from on high.

Thus our vanity, our self-love, promotes the cult of the genius: for only if we think of him as being very remote from us, as a miraculum, does he not aggrieve us...

But aside from these suggestions of our vanity, the activity of the genius seems in no way fundamentally different from the activity of the inventor of machines, the scholar of astronomy or history, the master of tactics.

All these activities are explicable if one pictures to oneself people whose thinking is active in one direction, who employ everything as material, who always zealously observe their own inner life and that of others, who perceive everywhere models and incentives, who never tire of combining together the means available to them.

Genius too does nothing but learn first how to lay bricks then how to build, and continually seek for material and continually form itself around it. Every activity of man is amazingly complicated, not only that of the genius: but none is a 'miracle.'"[1]

---

[1]Robert Greene, Mastery (London: Profile Books, 2012)

CHAPTER SUMMARY

- Investing is not easy, but it is simple.

- Investors get things wrong plenty of times; the urge to quit is always strong some days even with momentary gains.

- However, most times, hindrances are self-made and not external forces working against the investment progress.

- Work on your mindset, belief systems, and thought patterns.

- There are many investment philosophies from TechnoFunda to momentum and growth investment strategies; however, it is an investor's dedication to execution, understanding, and beliefs in the endeavor that brings results, not the investment philosophy.

- According to Malcolm Gladwell's supposition in his book Outliers, it takes approximately 10,000 hours to master one craft - that is approximately five years.

- While the mastery duration is not set in stone, the analogy goes to show it takes time, patience, determination, and resilience to master any craft - including investment.

- Investors must master their investment style; many investors ignore this principle and then blame the system when they fail.

- Believe in your abilities - prepare and implement the lessons from your investment journey.

- It is also crucial for investors to trust the process and strive for excellence.

- Charlie Munger rightly stated, "More important than the will to win is the will to prepare."

- Friedrich Nietzsche shared insights on the disbelief in capabilities; he asserts humans are too quick to dismiss perfection as odds, accidents, or supernatural gifts when they are humanly achievable.

- People create outliers out of success, talent, and achievers because it is only through distancing from such excellence that they avoid aggravation.

- However, perfection and excellence are a product of zeal. Even genius people lay the foundation early on once they become familiar with their abilities.

- Investors must hone their investing style - that is their craft and it comes with a lot of practice.

YOUR REFLECTIONS

(Reflect on what you have learned and pen down your thoughts)

_____

_____

_____

_____

_____

_____

_____

_____

_____

_____

_____

_____

_____

_____

_____

_____

_____

_____

_____

CHAPTER TWENTY

COMPOUNDING BEYOND MONEY

"More than your salary. More than the size of your house. More than the prestige of your job. Control over doing what you want, when you want to, with the people you want to, is the broadest lifestyle variable that makes people happy."
—Morgan Housel[1]

Many investors just run behind money during their investing journey and forget the true purpose of life. Money is just a means to achieve time freedom. It's an enabler to help us become the best version of ourselves.

Each of us gets a gift of 86,400 seconds every single day. And at the end of the day, it's gone. Imagine what would you have done if this was costing you, say ₹ 86,400 each day,

---

[1] Morgan Housel, *The Psychology of Money: Timeless Lessons on Wealth, Greed, and Happiness* (United Kingdom: Harriman House, 2020)

would you spend your time the same way? If the answer is "no", we need to look in the mirror and ask ourselves: what can I do to live each second in a fulfilled way?

"The rich invest in time, the poor invest in money."

— *Warren Buffett*

Compounding applies to habits, knowledge, goodwill, networks and experience. Each activity, every single thought, every second of our life compounds.

As soon as we think that we will do it tomorrow, let's compromise just for today, the game is already lost. In 2005, Steve Jobs gave a powerful thought during his Stanford commencement speech, he said, "When I was 17, I read a quote that went something like: "If you live each day as if it was your last, someday you'll most certainly be right." It made an impression on me, and since then, for the past 33 years, I have looked in the mirror every morning and asked myself: "If today were the last day of my life, would I want to do what I am about to do today?" And whenever the answer has been "No" for too many days in a row, I know I need to change something."[2]

Bottom line: Life is too short to delay working towards your passion, something you care about, something you always wanted to achieve. Start now, seize this moment. No excuses.

As Warren Buffett has said, "Chains of habit are too light to be felt until they are too heavy to be broken"[3]

---

[2]https://news.stanford.edu/2005/06/14/jobs-061505/
[3]https://www.brainyquote.com/quotes/warren_buffett_384858

Small incremental progressive steps in life can create magical compounding. Unfortunately, people underestimate the power of small consistent steps. This can be understood when we consider the contrast mis-reaction tendency in psychology.

Simply reading a few pages daily, a few minutes of daily exercise, spending quality time with loved ones, regularly doing charity and giving back, taking action towards your long-term goals, regular saving and investing - doing these regularly can improve your life multi-fold.

One of the best habits an investor can develop is that of writing. I see most of my friends in the trading community maintain a trading journal. But very few people maintain an investing journal. So, it is very important to maintain your own journal and focus on how you can improvise it. What is the residual risk that is embedded into the system? You must be very granular because what you measure is what matters. If you don't measure it, if you don't analyze it, it doesn't matter to you and if portfolio returns don't matter to you, you will never create wealth. You need to reflect on your actions, and then continuously improve your thought process.

Gautam Baid writes- "Carry a notebook and track all of your important decisions. A decision journal helps you collect accurate and honest feedback on what you were thinking when you made decisions. This feedback helps you realize when you were just plain lucky. Sometimes things work out well for very different reasons than we initially envisaged. The key to understanding the limits to our knowledge is to check the results of our decisions against what we thought was going to happen and why we thought it was going to happen."[4]

For example, many investors would have bought Eicher Motors for the commercial vehicle business, but the money ended up being made due to the two-wheeler motorcycle segment. Similarly, many investors might have bought Titan for the watch business, but the real cash cow ended up being the jewelry business. Thus, noting your reasons for buying and later reflecting is a powerful way to create a feedback loop and refine the process.

Noting our decisions and thought processes helps us overcome the intuitive feeling of "I knew it all along", known as the hindsight bias. The ideal way to do this is pen-and-paper, especially as we cannot deny our own handwriting. Alternatives include emailing or messaging a friend/ colleague/mentor/relative and reflecting on that.[5]

Becoming the best version of ourselves and unleashing our peak potential:

1. **First think of where we want to reach.** It's like setting a goal. Decide what is the best version of yourself. Use affirmations and tell yourself that you can do it.

2. **Choose that one thing that you can make your Ikigai (a reason for being).** Choose one task where you have passion and talent, it is something the world needs, and that people are willing to pay for. Focus.

---

[4]Gautam Baid, *The Joys of Compounding* (New York, Columbia University Press, 2020)
[5]https://malharmanek.wordpress.com/2021/08/29/on-overcoming-psychological-biases/

Once you find your true Ikigai, you will realize what you do is not work, it is enjoyment. It is not effort, it is fun.

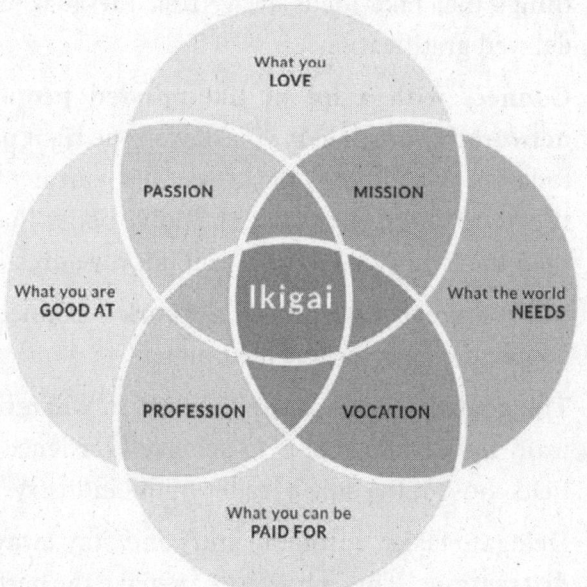

(https://www.forbes.com/sites/chrismyers/2018/02/23/how-to-find-your-ikigai-and-transform-your-outlook-on-life-and-business/?sh=33f093102ed4)

3. Once you have focused on the goal of **becoming the best version of yourself,** then learn the tools to achieve your goal. Implement these tools because knowledge without implementation is not knowledge. As Yogi Berra has said, "In theory, **there is no difference between theory and practice** - in practice there is."[6]

---

[6]https://www.brainyquote.com/quotes/yogi_berra_141506

4. **Focus on how I can solve problems** and not on how I can earn. Learning first, earning second.

5. **Create processes that will develop good habits.** Avoid things that take focus away from the goal. Choose delayed gratification.

6. **Connect with a lot of like-minded people and network.** This will help you stay on the right path. In today's day and age, your network is your net worth. If you surround yourself with people better than you, then the logical outcome is you improve drastically.

7. **Build a great distribution network** – connect with people through various mediums.

8. **The goal should be to be the best in whatever you want to be.** The goal is to achieve excellence in the field chosen. Become a leader in the industry.

9. **Delegate tasks, automate stuff and stay away from distractions.** This is how we can make the best of the most important asset. Time. As the quote says, "Life is too short to do everything by yourself."

10. **Longevity** – Focus on Goals or design goals in sectors that will stay long term. Build bonds with people who think farsightedly. Be adaptive and be relevant. Humans are inherently obsessed with the short term. We always overestimate what we can achieve in the short term, but underestimate what we can achieve eventually. Thinking about the long term rather than the near term is a sure way to get an edge over the rest of the crowd. Jeff Bezos said, "If everything you do needs to work on a three-year time horizon, then

you're competing against a lot of people. But if you're willing to invest on a seven-year time horizon, you're now competing against a fraction of those people, because very few companies are willing to do that. Just by lengthening the time horizon, you can engage in endeavors that you could never otherwise pursue."[7]

11. **Selling is the most important thing.** Selling is not a bad thing. Don't shy away from learning to sell. It's a good service for the world. Without sales, great products/services will never reach those who need them. As Naval Ravikant said, "Learn to sell, learn to build, if you can do both, you will be unstoppable."[8]

12. **Cutting Out the Noise:** Most of what we hear is not signal, but noise. Even during all the crises, eventually, the market bounces back. So never get too pessimistic during any crash.

---

[7]https://www.goodreads.com/quotes/7648364-if-everything-you-do-needs-to-work-on-a-three-year#:~:text=Quotes%20%3E%20Quotable%20Quote-,%E2%80%9CIf%20everything%20you%20do%20-needs%20to%20work%20on%20a%20three,a%20fraction%20of%20those%20people%E2%80%A6

[8]https://nav.al/build-sell

Panic stations

Impact of global crises on Dow Jones

Event	Reaction dates	No. of days it hit lows	Change (%)	% change 3 mths	% change 6 mths	% change 1 yr
Germany defeats the French	May 9, 1940 - Jun 22, 1940	13	-17.1	+8.4	+7.0	-5.2
Pearl Harbour attack	Dec 6, 1941 - Dec 10, 1941	4	-6.5	-2.9	-9.6	-5.4
Korean War	Jun 23, 1950 - Jul 13, 1950	20	-12.0	+15.3	+19.2	+26.3
Sputnick	Oct 3, 1957 - Oct 22, 1957	19	-9.9	+6.7	+7.2	+29.2
Cuban Missile Crisis	Oct 19, 1962 - Oct 27, 1962	8	-1.1	+17.1	+24.2	+30.4
JFK assassination	Nov 21, 1963 - Nov 22, 1963	1	-2.9	+12.4	+15.1	+24.0
US bombs Cambodia	Apr 29, 1970 - May 26, 1970	27	-14.4	+20.3	+20.7	+43.7
Arab oil embargo	Oct 18, 1973 - Dec 5, 1973	49	-17.9	+10.2	+7.2	-25.5
Nixon resigns	Aug 9, 1974 - Aug 29, 1974	20	-15.5	-5.7	+12.5	+27.2
USSR in Afghanistan	Dec 24, 1979 - Jan 3, 1980	22	-2.2	-4.0	+6.8	+21.0
Hunt silver crash	Feb 13, 1980 - Mar 27, 1980	45	-15.9	+16.2	+25.8	+30.6
US bombs Libya	Apr 15, 1986 - Apr 21, 1986	6	-2.6	-4.1	-1.0	+25.9
1987 stock market crash	Oct 2, 1987 - Oct 19, 1987	17	-34.2	+11.4	+15.0	+24.2
Iraq invades Kuwait	Feb 8, 1990 - Aug 23, 1990	21	-13.3	+2.3	+16.3	+22.4
Gulf War ultimatum	Dec 24, 1990 - Jan 16, 1991	23	-4.3	+19.8	+18.7	+24.5
Gorbachev coup	Aug 16, 1991 - Aug 19, 1991	3	-2.4	+1.6	+11.3	+14.9
World Trade Centre (car bombing)	Apr 18, 1995 - Apr 20, 1995	2	-0.3	+5.1	+8.5	+14.2
Oklahoma City bombing	Apr 19, 1995 - Apr 20, 1995	1	+0.6	+9.7	+12.9	+30.8
Asian crisis	Oct 7, 1997 - Oct 27, 1997	20	-12.4	+10.5	+25.0	+16.9
US embassy bombs Africa	Aug 7, 1998 - Aug 10, 1998	3	-0.3	+4.7	+6.5	+25.8
Russian & long-term capital crisis	Aug 18, 1998 - Oct 8, 1998	50	-11.3	+24.7	+33.7	+37.7
September 11 attacks	Sep 11, 2001 - Sep 21, 2001	5	-16.0	+24.4	+30.0	-1.0
Lehman Brothers collapse	Sep 29, 2008 - Nov 21, 2008	40	-33.0	-1.1	+11.3	+40.2
GFC peak fear	Feb 9, 2009 - Mar 6, 2009	20	-21.7	+35.6	+46.0	+63.0
Flash crash	May 6, 2010 - May 21, 2010	12	-8.7	+1.0	+12.9	+26.0
Japanese tsunami	Mar 11, 2011 - Mar 16, 2011	4	-4.1	+3.5	-0.4	+14.5
Fears about China's economy	Jul 28, 2015 - Aug 24, 2015	20	-15.1	+15.9	+7.2	+20.0
Recession fears (Fed rate hikes)	Dec 4, 2018 - Dec 24, 2018	14	-15.5	+17.1	+22.6	+31.0
World closes down due to COVID-19	Feb 20, 2020 - Mar 23, 2020	23	-34.8	+44.0	+47.0	+78.0
Average of all events		**18**	**-11.6**	**+11.1**	**+15.2**	**+24.7**

The market corrects in expectation of a crisis and rallies during the crisis.[9]

*(https://blog.abakkusinvest.com/wp-content/
uploads/2022/02/Market-Outlook-Views-on-Current-
Events-Feb-2022.pdf)*

---

[9]https://www.reddit.com/r/Damnthatsinteresting/comments/t059g7/
impact_of_global_crises_on_dow_jones

13. **Keep reinvesting in yourself.** This is the most important thing. Dividend equals giving something to yourself. Use this as a positive feedback loop. Ask for feedback and keep improving. To quote Charlie Munger- "I constantly see people rise in life who are not the smartest, sometimes not even the most diligent, but they are learning machines. They go to bed every night a little wiser than they were when they got up and boy does that help, particularly when you have a long run ahead of you."[10]

POWER OF SMALL INCREMENTAL STEPS - THE KAIZEN WAY

In life and investing, we see bigger goals and give up at the initial stage thinking they will be impossible to achieve. But the secret to achieving your goals, becoming a better version, to be successful, is to take small incremental steps - consistently.

Kaizen is a Japanese technique that means "taking small steps for continual improvement." *One Small Step Can Change Your Life: The Kaizen Way* by Robert Maurer is a powerful book that covers this concept. It talks about how taking small incremental steps can make a big difference in one's life.

In his book, Robert Maurer talks about six strategies that can help us bring about big changes in our life by taking small incremental steps consistently for a long time:

---

[10]https://learnrepeatacademy.com/charlie-munger-quotes/

1. Asking small questions

2. Thinking small thoughts

3. Taking small actions

4. Solving small problems

5. Giving small rewards

6. Recognizing small moments

This is a powerful mental model which each one of us should follow in our life and investing journey to compound every aspect to achieve great results.

"The journey of a thousand miles begins with a single step."

—Lao Tzu

COMPOUND YOUR KARMA

"Life is an echo. What you send out, comes back.
What you sow, you reap. What you give, you get.
What you see in others, exists in you.

Remember, life is an echo. It always gets back to you.

So, give goodness."

—Zig Ziglar

We all know about Newton's third law of motion which simply means - that to every action, there will always be an equal and opposite reaction. Life works in the same way through the "Law of Karma" - what goes around comes around.

Unfortunately, most schools only teach theories that will only make us employable. But life is beyond that. Each action is like a seed, we reap what we sow. Let's do good deeds, give back to society, have good intentions, have the right thoughts, be kind and respect others.

Stephen Covey wrote, "You are free to make whatever choice you want, but you are not free from the consequences of the choice."

In one beautiful passage about his autobiography, Ed Viesturs, a high-altitude mountaineer, wrote, "Although I remain uncertain about God or any particular religion, I believe in karma. What goes around, comes around. How you live your life, the respect that you give others and the mountain, and how you treat people, in general, will come back to you in a kindred fashion. I like to talk about what I call the Karma National Bank. If you give up the summit to help rescue someone who is in trouble, you've put a deposit in that bank. And sometime down the road, you may need to make a big withdrawal."

Let's keep doing good deeds and keep compounding balance in our Karma Bank. This is true compounding, this is the true meaning of life.

FINAL THOUGHTS:

Financial Freedom is possible for each one of you when you thoughtfully build the Mega Compounding Machine for yourself by saving, investing and implementing the system. Have positive intentions, keep learning, stay in the game, respect risk, be humble and do good karma. India is a land of opportunities, so be prepared to grab these opportunities - find them, ride them. May the force be with you.

As Aryan said the last words, the trio noticed sun rays leaking through a gap in the curtains. Silence punctuated for a couple of moments. For the couple, it was like basking in the sunbeams of enlightenment. At the same time, they were shellshocked, as they had spent a long time in the bubble of ignorance, battling with their finances.

Chatur and Ranjita thanked Aryan for sharing his wisdom with them and also promised him to transform their learnings into action.

And, a new day, a new life blossomed thereafter.

You too can compound! All the best.

CHAPTER SUMMARY

- According to Morgan Housel, if you want to be happy, you should gain control of the things you do, how you do them, and the people you do them with - control is the solution.

- There is more to life than making money - there is also living.

- Money is simply a means of reaching time freedom.

- Make the most out of the gift of time; there are 86,400 seconds worth investing in living.

- Each second, action, and thought in life compounds.

- Procrastination is the enemy of time.

- Life is short; therefore, make every moment count - carpe diem.

- Journaling is an essential aspect of investment; it provides an unbiased source of data for the investor, brings thought structure, and impacts the endeavor's success.

- Make habits out of gainful experiences; Warren Buffett said it well, "Chains of habit are too light to be felt until they are too heavy to be broken."

- Tiny incremental steps eventually compound into big moves; never underestimate the power of small beginnings and consistency.

- The first step to living to your full potential is setting your goal to determine where you want to reach.

- Prioritize your passion and talent in the goal establishment.
- Learn the tools to achieve the set goal.
- Focus on problem-solving rather than earnings first.
- Learn beneficial habits that steer you toward the goal.
- Interact with like-minded people and have interactions across different mediums.
- Aim for excellence as you work to achieve this goal.
- Streamline and automate tasks; you can also capitalize on delegation.
- Always focus on the long-term when building relationships, developing tasks, or determining the main goal.
- Be comfortable with selling; it is a natural necessary practice.
- Eliminate the noise; it is always a distraction.
- Keep reinventing yourself.
- Robert Maurer provides six strategies for making small incremental steps: asking small questions, thinking small thoughts, thinking small actions, solving small problems, giving small rewards, and recognizing small moments.
- You reap what you sow and every action has an equal reaction; therefore, be prepared to face the consequences of your actions.

YOUR REFLECTIONS

(Reflect on what you have learned and pen down your thoughts)

_____

_____

_____

_____

_____

_____

_____

_____

_____

_____

_____

_____

_____

_____

_____

_____

_____

_____

_____

_____

10 POWERFUL INVESTING AFFIRMATIONS

1. I Earn Massive Passive Income. I am Financially Free

2. I have a choice. I work because I choose to, not because I have to

3. I admire and Model Rich and Successful People

4. I am Truly Grateful for all Money and Knowledge that I have

5. I am committed to constantly learning. I take Investing seriously

6. I always follow my system and remain objective at all times

7. I always avoid noise and distractions

8. I always Respect Risk

9. I think and act in my long-term interest

10. I am a Mega Compounding Machine

To Download these Affirmations in HD Poster Format:

https://TechnoFunda.co/affirmations

FURTHER READING RECOMMENDATIONS

Find my latest list of recommended books on Amazon:

http://technofunda.co/books

ACKNOWLEDGEMENTS

I would like to thank my family for supporting me in my investing journey and motivating me to write this book. Also, I would like to extend my special thanks to Malhar Manek who helped me in articulating this book. Finally, my gratitude to all my mentors, investor friends and TechnoFunda Investing Community for helping me become a lifelong learner of markets.

Gratitude to my dear friend , author and coach Som Bathla, from whom I could learn writing this book. Thanks to entire Penman publishing team for helping me publish this book.

My sincere thanks and all credits to Tradingview for all the technical charts shared in this book.

ENDNOTES

I know that investing is a wide subject and a lot of data points can keep changing from time to time. I am committed to making changes to the references as needed in the future.

I would also like to acknowledge that I may have made a mistake in this book - either in attributing something incorrectly or not giving credit to someone inadvertently. If you find any such case, please email me at *connect@ vivekmashrani.com* and I would be happy to fix it as soon as possible.

Scan QR code to access the
Penguin Random House India website